The
Book *of* Hope

The
Book *of* Hope

Meditations for Passion
Power and Promise

Eileen Campbell

S

This edition first published in Great Britain in 2018 by Orion Spring,
an imprint of the Orion Publishing Group Ltd
Carmelite House, 50 Victoria Embankment,
London, EC4Y 0DZ
An Hachette UK Company

1 3 5 7 9 10 8 6 4 2

DISCLAIMER

*The information in this book is not in any way a substitute for receiving conventional medical
treatment or consulting a physician. All the practices in this book are to be used as an addition to
existing treatments to assist the healing process and should be fully explored only in conjunction
with suitable training. Neither the author nor the publisher assumes any liability at all for
any damage caused through the application or misapplication of procedures and statements
contained in this book.*

A CIP catalogue record for this book
is available from the British Library.

ISBN: 9781409177883

Contents

Chapter 2 · Having conviction and holding on to our ideals 31

Chapter 3 · Daring to take action 65

Chapter 4 · Persevering when it's an uphill struggle 91

Chapter 5 · Cultivating patience   121

Chapter 6 · Opening our hearts to love 159

Chapter 7 · Growing in wisdom 189

Chapter 8 · Becoming our best selves 219

Introduction

We live in dangerous and uncertain times, lurching from one crisis to the next and reeling from one tragedy after another. We crave certainty, but life is in essence unpredictable. Hope appears to be in short supply, and fear can so easily overwhelm us as we try to stay afloat in our sea of troubles. In our personal lives, as in our dysfunctional world, we cannot protect ourselves from being touched by suffering. There is no cure for being part of the human race, and this can sometimes leave us feeling hopeless and powerless. We can all too easily find ourselves in a dark place of despair, reacting with anger or blame, or attempting to insulate or even anesthetize ourselves against the pain.

In Greek mythology when Pandora lifted the lid of the box she had been forbidden to open, all kinds of evil spirits were let loose into the world to wreak havoc. At the same time, however, a healing spirit named Hope was released to help humanity deal with suffering.

However dark the situation, hope is always available to us—"hope springs eternal in the human breast," wrote the poet Alexander Pope. Hope is born in darkness, just as we see the stars only when the sky is black.

Crisis isn't totally bad, however; it can result in breakthrough as well as breakdown. Hope doesn't deny the darkness, nor does it expect everything to be as it once was before the crisis, but it does offer the possibility of redemption. Quite simply, hope is a miracle for it changes us, changes the situation we find ourselves in, and is contagious, spreading beyond us to others.

Hope is both a choice and an action. If we give way to despair, we are unable to do anything. And although human history is a catalog of woes, it is worth reminding ourselves that it is also rich with magnanimous acts of courage, sacrifice, and compassion.

The Book of Hope

We need to practice being hopeful and making good things happen, focusing on what we long for and taking determined steps to bring it about. What we put into practice becomes habit. When we shift our perspective and face the pain we feel, things begin to look different. Not only do we find ourselves surviving, but we also become empowered. We learn that the very things that have caused us to suffer and despair are the experiences that contribute to our growth and maturity. Crisis asks of us to bring forth the best of ourselves and use what talents we have to help others. In daring to take action, we trust that there is the possibility that what we contribute can make a difference.

So what steps can we take in the face of pain and suffering to access hope and make our own lives happier and help to spread hope to others?

First and foremost, we need vision and conviction that the future can be better. When we believe this, we are motivated to act with bravery and daring. If we're determined, we can drive through our vision, but being patient and letting things unfold without trying to force them are also necessary for balance. Instead of being afraid of the future and closing down, we can open our hearts and feel a profound sense of connection to others. We empower ourselves, and, as our capacity for self-awareness increases, we grow in wisdom. As each one of us changes, becoming the best we can be, so our world is transformed.

Throughout the book, I include stories of those who have triumphed over adversity and been sustained by hope: survivors of holocaust, exile, and imprisonment, for example—Anne Frank, Malala Yousafzai, Shirin Ebadi; social activists—Grace Lee Boggs, Harriet Tubman, Wangari Maathai; explorers and extreme adventurers—Ann Davison, Sacagawea, Diana Nyad; scientists like Marie Curie; artists, composers, poets, and writers—Artemisia Gentileschi, Hildegard of Bingen, Emily Dickinson, and Xiaolu Guo. I also include the experiences of those who have been abused or kidnapped—Maya Angelou, Oprah Winfrey, and Natascha Kampusch; and the stories of refugees who have made new lives for themselves, escaping from Uganda, Iran, and Syria.

I write from my own experience of facing difficulties. Like you perhaps, I know what it is to have had a difficult start in life; to have struggled financially; to have experienced betrayal, disappointment, and divorce; to have been seriously ill and wondered whether I would recover; to have lost family members and friends; to know what failure feels like; to have been attacked and injured by someone with mental illness; to have had my home burgled; and to have experienced a degree of trauma—I was close to the World Trade Center in New York on 9/11 and flew into Nepal the day of the 2015 earthquake. Yet, I know that all these experiences, however painful and difficult they've been, have helped me grow. When with reflection I realized I had a choice about being hopeful or not, I discovered that I had greater resilience than I ever imagined. I found greater meaning and purpose in my life because of what I had been through, and as a result am now happier and more fulfilled, and feel grateful for all that life offers me.

I hope that whatever hardships and difficulties you are struggling with in your life, *The Book of Hope* will help you see the issues with greater clarity and that you choose hope and discover new depths of understanding on your journey, ultimately finding a sense of peace and joy.

The
Book *of* Hope

Chapter 1

Creating our vision of the future

*The point about hope is that it is something that
occurs in very dark moments. It is like a flame
in the darkness.*

—JOHN BERGER

Each of us at some point in our lives is likely to experience adversity, grief, and despair. For some, the crisis may follow the loss of a loved one, an accident, an illness, or an unexpected firing or dismissal. It may be an ongoing struggle with poverty or abuse, or it could be simply the dire state of the world with its inequality, violence, and terrorism that plunges us into a deep depression.

Whatever the cause, hope seems to elude us, and fear, doubt, and confusion make us lose our way. We reach rock bottom. This is sometimes referred to as a "dark night of the soul," originating from the title of a poem by sixteenth-century Spanish mystic and poet St. John of the Cross. On such occasions it's hard to see any light at the end of the tunnel, we feel overwhelmed by the darkness, and the future stretches bleakly before us. We find ourselves questioning the whole basis of our lives and whether there is any meaning and purpose in them.

Hope is the opposite of despair, and we need it because it helps us deal with our suffering, but how is it possible to coax hope from the embers of despair? We can start by reminding ourselves that the light is always there, even though we can't at the moment see it. There is never a time when dawn doesn't break or winter doesn't end. Hope is like the bird singing in the dark night, sensing the approach of the dawn light. When we accept that light is the other side of darkness, we are more able to face our dilemma. Nothing stays the same forever—things change, we change. We can turn things around and begin again, perhaps making something good out of the pain and turmoil we feel.

It may well take some time to accept and come to terms with what has brought us to this juncture, but that glimmer of hope in the darkness helps us find resources that we didn't know we possessed. We discover a different perspective that helps us deal with the situation. As Maya Angelou, the American poet, writer, and social rights activist, put so well, "God puts rainbows in the clouds so that each of us—in the dreariest and most dreaded moments—can see a possibility of hope."

Once we have tasted hope, we can hold on to it, magnifying it while building a vision of something better. Hope makes the present less difficult to bear and gives us the energy to pursue our dream. Our dark night has been like a death and a rebirth, an awakening to a greater sense of meaning and purpose. Each new day we can cultivate a more expansive state of mind and enrich our lives with the prospect of a brighter future, one in which the essence of who we truly are is revealed, as spoken of by the Persian Sufi poet Hafiz:

> I wish I could show you,
> When you are lonely or in darkness,
> The Astonishing Light
> Of your own Being!

Creating our vision of the future

1. Turning things around

Let's imagine we've allowed the possibility of hope to surface. Perhaps the future can look different. Maybe all is not lost.

There's a story about a famous painting called *The Chess Players* (sometimes also called *Checkmate* and *The Game of Life*) by Friedrich Moritz August Retzsch. Probably painted in 1831, it used to hang in a public gallery but is now in private hands. The painting depicts two people playing chess, one of whom is Satan, the other a young man, possibly Faust, since Retzsch illustrated Goethe's *Faust*.

The chessboard appears to be placed on the lid of a sarcophagus, and a skull reminds us that death is never far away. Hope is also present in the form of a guardian angel, who watches over the young man. He looks forlorn, as if he knows the game is over and his soul is lost. Checkmate!

The story goes that a chess Grandmaster on a visit to the gallery spent a long time studying the positions of the chess pieces. Suddenly he cried out, "It's a lie. The painter is wrong. There is a way out. The king has another move." The young man actually has the chance to defeat his deadly opponent. All is not lost!

However desperate a situation and however troubled we may feel, there is always hope. Just as stars in the sky are at their brightest when it's truly dark, so we can find hope in the darkness of despair. Whatever our pain and suffering, all is not lost. We have a choice; we can save ourselves: we can select hope and turn the situation around.

I remind myself that there is always hope, however dark things may seem.
I am choosing hope and turning the situation around.
I know that I possess the resources to deal with my problem.

2. Allowing inspiration to take hold

If we choose to rise above our circumstances and dare to hope that the future might be better, we need to feel inspired and focus on what lifts our spirits, rather than be brought down by the negative messages and depressing news stories that dominate our media. We need positive and hopeful encouragement. After all, as the Dalai Lama reminds us:

The very purpose of our life is happiness, which is sustained by hope. We have no guarantee about the future, but we exist in the hope of something better. Hope means keeping going, thinking, "I can do this." It brings inner strength, self-confidence, the ability to do what you do honestly, truthfully and transparently.

We actually have a tool we can use to help us, one that is always with us—our breath. *Inspire* means to breathe into or blow upon, so inspiration is breathing into the mind or soul. Instead of focusing on those thoughts that make us feel hopeless, we can choose to focus on our breath instead. This simple act of connecting with the breath calms us and helps us feel more hopeful. As the basis of meditation and as a regular practice (see pp. 50–51), it can have enormously beneficial effects.

We can also turn to nature to inspire us. Modern life has somehow caused us to become disconnected from nature, yet we can choose to take a walk in a park or garden, along a river or canal, by the sea-shore—wherever we can take ourselves to so that we can be aware of the beauty of our surroundings. Allowing our senses to be uplifted by nature's sights, sounds, and scents enables us to forget our troubles for a while and recharges our batteries.

We might choose to listen to some uplift-ing music, go for a swim, have a massage, read an inspirational book, look at paintings in a gallery, cook something special, or do some gardening. Sometimes merely taking a long luxurious bath, washing our hair, and putting on fresh clothes and make-up can make a difference to our mood.

Affirmations help too, by changing our patterns of thought, feeling, and behavior. An affirmation is a strong positive statement, which can be general or specific. It has to be clear and concise and in the present tense, as if it already exists. We can affirm, for example: "The future looks brighter for me" rather than "The future will be brighter for me." We can say the affirmations silently or out loud, or we can write them down. Making continuous positive statements and trying to believe an affirmation as much as possible helps shake off any negativity and restore some kind of balance in ourselves. While accepting what currently exists, we can see the possibility of creating something better for the future and therefore feel energized and more hopeful, even in the most difficult of situations.

I dare to hope the future is brighter.
Focusing on my breath, I am calmer and more
balanced.
I seek to be nourished and inspired.

Creating our vision of the future
....

3. Vibrating at a higher frequency

Our universe consists of matter and energy. Matter is merely energy moving very slowly, which behaves at a quantum level like a wave. Energy is matter moving very rapidly, and it takes the form of a field with invisible lines of force. The universe is a constant translation of matter into energy and energy into matter, which is expressed through vibrations, waves, and fields. Everything in the universe vibrates, including us, and our emotions are also vibrations.

When we choose to hope rather than despair, we automatically tune in to a higher vibrational level, freeing ourselves from the negative impact of the slower vibrations like fear, anxiety, and doubt. We don't have to be held back by self-limiting thoughts and ideas that have become ingrained and that tell us something isn't possible. We can change them.

Neuroscience has shown that we create our world moment by moment with our thoughts, words, and deeds, something the truly wise have always known and that are expressed here in the words of the Buddha:

The thought manifests as the word
The word manifests as the deed
The deed develops into habit

And the habit hardens into character.

We can envision and create better lives for ourselves through accessing the higher vibrational states of imagination, insight, and intuition. To develop these states, we need a greater balance of the right and left hemispheres of the brain. Most of us tend to be left-brain dominant, relying on it for rational thinking and our actions and responses to events in our lives. There's nothing wrong with rational thinking, but sometimes we don't know all the facts, or a situation is gray or confused because of too many facts, and that's where intuitive skills are more helpful. It's the right brain that is more attuned to these. Even a great scientist like Einstein recognized that intuition is important. All of us have intuitive abilities, but we just need to practice using them more.

We can develop our intuition by changing the way we pay attention in the world. Technology has brought so many distractions that our attention is focused on what is going on outside and around us, rather than what is going on in our inner world. We tend not to trust the signs, gut feelings, coincidences, or our dreams—those sources of information that come from our subconscious mind and are there to help us on our journey. Intuition gives us a different way of perceiving the world and helps us see what's hard to see. It can tell us what's right and wrong in our lives, what we need to change, and where we need to make adjustments.

When we access both right and left sides of the brain, we're less trapped by the problems we find ourselves facing. We're connected to the life force and attuned to the higher vibrations, enabling us to eliminate those attitudes and behaviors that keep us stuck.

However difficult the circumstances of our lives, hope and despair are both attitudes experienced by our minds. When we choose to bring the higher vibration of hope to a situation, we find things begin to shift and change.

I let go of fear, anxiety, and doubt.
I create my world moment by moment, envisioning a
*   better life for myself.*
I choose to use my intuition to perceive the world
*   differently.*

4. Dreaming the impossible dream

What is it we most long for? Most of us want good relationships, a comfortable home, a rewarding career, good health, but probably much more besides—and there's nothing wrong with that! We're all entitled to dream, we don't need permission, and neither do we have to prove anything. Basically, we want what will make us happy. Sometimes, however, we have a burning desire to do something that may seem impossible and that others might regard as a foolish dream. We have to take that passionate desire and make it our quest, no matter how difficult it might seem to reach our goal.

Dreams are expressions of hope, and how our lives unfold depends on our dreams. When our imagination is fired by them, we're lifted to new heights, and we can overcome those patterns of thoughts and beliefs that so frequently hold us back and prevent us from realizing our dream.

"The future belongs to those who believe in the beauty of their dreams," wrote Eleanor Roosevelt, who in spite of her privileged position as the wife of US President Franklin D. Roosevelt had her share of misfortunes and is to be admired for how she coped with them. She campaigned throughout her life for human rights and as head of the United Nations Commission on Human Rights helped draft the 1948 declaration of human rights.

Doreen Peachy did not have a privileged background, but she had dreams. When she grew up in the 1950s in England, there wasn't enough money in her family to pay for ballet lessons, but she always wanted to be a ballerina. When she was seventy-one, she became the oldest woman ever to pass the grade six exam at the Royal Academy of Dance in London. Having had a successful career, she was able to fulfill her dream by taking up ballet when she had retired ten years earlier.

My own experience with singing is not dissimilar. I always loved to sing, but there was no money for music training when I was young. I put all my energy into getting an education and a career, and it never really occurred to me that I could take up singing without a music background, but the dream never left me. It was not until I was fifty, after many years of going to India, that through a curious serendipity I became involved with classical Indian raga. Indian music and the way it is traditionally taught, totally by listening and by repetition with no need for musical notation, suited me perfectly. Because I had studied Sanskrit, singing in different Indian languages wasn't really a problem; I seemed to be able to pick them up enough to be able to sing in them. After many years of practice now, learning different styles with several Indian teachers, I have become reasonably proficient, even performing on stage in both London and India. It's clearly never too late to fulfill an impossible dream!

I allow my imagination to run free.
I know that what I long for is attainable.
I believe my dreams are being realized.

5. Saying "yes" to possibility

With all its uncertainty and unpredictability, life may be challenging for us at times, but it's always richer with possibilities than we might at first think. We always have a choice as to how we react to situations. If we remain hopeful, open, and receptive, the future unfolds in a manner that allows us to pursue and realize our dreams. Possibilities emerge that, if we're negative and despairing in our attitude, we fail to see.

Throughout history there have sadly been exiles and refugees, and recent history has been no exception with the turmoil in the Middle East. We have all been appalled by the plight of thousands of refugees leaving the horrors of war-torn Syria to come to the West. One of the most heart-rending, but at the same time inspirational, stories is that of the young girl Nujeen Mustafa, who has cerebral palsy and cannot walk. She traveled in her wheelchair in search of a new life, wanting to join her brother and sister in Germany, and dreaming of becoming an astronaut. From Bodrum in Turkey, she traveled in an overcrowded dingy to the Greek island of Lesbos and then took a fourteen-hour ferry ride to mainland Greece. The Hungarian/Serbian border had closed to refugees the day before her arrival, so she had to make a long detour via Croatia and Slovenia, where she was held in a detention center for twenty-four hours, before finally making the long bus journey to Germany. Now settled and at school, she plans to go on to study physics. It was her positive attitude and saying "yes" to the possibility of safety and a new life that Nujeen believes helped her face the long and difficult journey: "I thought of it as something that I'm living through now, but that will pass. I thought of everything as a big adventure."

I have Gujarati friends living in England, who similarly had hopeful attitudes when they were expelled from Idi Amin's Uganda in August 1972. Of the eighty thousand Asians who were ordered to leave Uganda, thirty thousand came to the UK, leaving behind their wealth and possessions. They brought with them, however, a determination to rebuild their lives, no matter the sacrifices that had to be made.

They said "yes" to starting all over again, even though their start was hardly propitious—they were housed in old military camps with very few facilities. Their parents worked hard and they worked hard, studying to get more qualifications and build successful businesses. My friends' stories are stories of struggle, but one is a consultant anesthetist, another ran a successful chain of pharmacies before retiring, and another was an academic librarian. All are engaged in volunteer work in their communities. I'm full of admiration for how they overcame adversity and how they have built successful lives for themselves and are contributing to their communities too.

With a hopeful, determined attitude, however much things are against us at certain points in our lives, we can undoubtedly win when we say "yes" to the possibilities that are always there for us.

I am emerging from my difficult times.
I am hopeful, open, and receptive to a glorious future.
I say "yes" to the possibilities that are unfolding.

6. Finding meaning and purpose

Humans have a fundamental need to feel that life is worthwhile and that what we do makes a difference. We may be rich, successful, even famous, but that's not enough—we have to have a reason to live. It may well be easier for a camel to enter the eye of a needle than for a rich man to enter heaven! In the long run, without a meaningful existence, life is empty and unfulfilling.

To make sense of our existence, we need to see ourselves as part of something greater—a family, a community, a society. We need to seek a cause beyond ourselves, and it has to be worth making sacrifices for. Many find meaning through loving and caring for others or trying to have a beneficial impact on the lives of others. Ultimately, seeing ourselves as on a spiritual path makes the difference, and every life event—negative or positive—is a clue to our purpose and becoming our best selves. Rudolf Steiner, the founder of Anthroposophy and the Waldorf Schools, wrote:

> If we do not develop within ourselves this deeply rooted feeling that there is something higher than ourselves, we shall never find the strength to evolve to something higher.

There are many examples of those who have come to this realization in a variety of ways—from saint to sinner.

Mother Teresa, the founder of the Order of the Missionaries of Charity, was canonized as St. Teresa of Calcutta in 2016. In spite of intense inner struggles on her spiritual journey for much of her life, Mother Teresa found meaning and purpose through her work with the poor, the sick, and the dying. She was unwavering in her dedication to helping and giving hope to those in need. "Love cannot remain by itself—it has no meaning," she wrote. "Love has to be put into action, and that action is service."

A very different story of hope is that of Moyo (a Swahili name meaning heart or spirit), who has been held on death row for the past sixteen years, having committed two murders when he was eighteen. He does not expect to be let out of solitary confinement, but his hope is to spend his time in worthwhile ways. In trying to understand himself and what happened, he has become an avid reader. He has committed himself to a regular practice of yoga and meditation. He says, "In this cell I have learned the art of patience, the art of silence, and its fruits are sweet. I have learned the art of introspection and what it can do to improve one's sense of self."

Moyo also communicates with the world outside through letters and met Maria Jain through a prison pen-pals initiative. The same age, but with very different lives, they began to meditate together sitting in their different time zones. Out of the deep friendship that developed came the exhibition titled "Buddhas on Death Row." When meditating in his cell one day, Moyo decided that he would like to study the image of the Buddha through a series of portraits. Maria helped organize an exhibition of his work at an art gallery in Helsinki. The portraits are accompanied by reflections on suffering and happiness, conflict and peace, impermanence and eternity, ignorance and awareness.

Moyo continues to be committed to the work of transformation. Instead of feeling anger and resentment, as he once did, he sees himself as working to "polish his soul, clean stains from his heart, and open windows of his mind." He has chosen to find meaning and purpose in his situation.

However dire the circumstances, there is always hope, as Moyo's story shows, not necessarily that the situation will end, but that the situation looks different. As human beings, we clearly have the capacity for transformation, even in the darkness, when we find a meaning and purpose to our existence.

I know that however difficult my situation is, hope is always available.

I am learning to make sense of my existence.
I spend my time in worthwhile ways.

7. Letting our creativity blossom

If we want to change our lives and create a future that's better than the situation we're currently experiencing, then we need to use our imagination to the full. Pir Vilyat Khan, the much-loved Sufi teacher, wrote: "The future is not there waiting for us. We create it by the power of the imagination."

We're all capable of accessing our imagination; it's just that as adults we don't necessarily employ it as easily as we did when we were children. We were more open and receptive then, but becoming adults meant that as we learned the ways of our left-brain-dominated culture, we probably became more closed down and inhibited.

Imagination is such a powerful tool when we give it free rein. It is connected with the life force, the source of all creativity, and we need to turn inward to find this so that inspiration floods in and increases our hope for what is possible. Instead of being perpetually drawn outward by all the distractions of modern life, if we pay attention to our inner world, we can more easily access imagination and picture (literally) new vistas and new ways of being. What we imagine, we can create, and the vision we create on the mental level, giving us a sense of purpose born of hope, can spur us on in our darkest moments.

Patanjali, the great exponent of yoga writing in the second century BC, understood the process:

> When you are inspired by some great purpose, some extraordinary project, all your thoughts break their bonds; your mind transcends limitations, your consciousness expands in every direction, and you find yourself in a new, great and wonderful world.

One of America's greatest poets, Emily Dickinson, had a rich interior life and lived in a world with far less stimulation than ours. Hers was a life of simplicity and seclusion in the family home in nineteenth-century Amherst, Massachusetts. "To live is so startling, it leaves little room for other occupations," she claimed. Along with the almost eighteen hundred poems she wrote, her life comprised baking, gardening, attending church, painting, reading books, playing the piano and singing, and taking walks. She shared her poems mainly with family and friends and was barely published in her lifetime. We know from both her poems and her letters that she suffered tragic losses among her family and friends, and she wrote about the nature of death and immortality with great power and insight. Unorthodox and independent in her views on religion, Emily drew inspiration from the beauty of nature and her experiences of ecstatic joy. She well understood the nature of hope, expressed in her famous lines:

> Hope is the thing with feathers
> That perches in the soul
> And sings the tune without the words
> And never stops at all.

We too can be in touch with our inner world and let our creativity blossom. When we're hopeful and open to receiving inspiration, our imagination is fired, ideas seem to come to us out of the blue, and we feel joyful and alive. We're affirming our creative nature and can put our energy into making the future brighter.

> *I turn inward to access the power of my imagination.*
> *I am putting my creative energy into making the future brighter.*
> *I find myself in a new and wonderful world.*

Creating our vision of the future

8. Living with integrity

One of the most important things for us to do when we want to change our lives for the better is to pay attention to the spiritual dimension of ourselves, just as much as we take care of the physical, mental, and emotional aspects. All four aspects of ourselves have to be part of the equation of the whole person that we are.

Having integrity is not about fitting in, pleasing others, telling lies, and modifying our behavior accordingly in order to achieve something. It's about living with the energies of the higher vibrations and being in touch with who we truly are. We are happier when we live our truth. The authentic self is naturally balanced and is the real source of self-esteem, courage, and imagination.

Living with integrity doesn't require us to have more time or more resources. We can begin exactly where we are. When we choose hope and commit to working to change the circumstances of our lives through altering our attitude and behavior, we begin to see the possibilities for things to be different and find the courage to pursue them.

Shirin Ebadi is an Iranian lawyer and was Iran's first female judge. With the Islamic Revolution of

1979, women were forbidden to judge men, so she was demoted and given a job with clerical duties instead. Rather than compromise her integrity, she resigned her post, and it was not until 1992 that she was able to set up her own practice. Unlike others, however, she did not leave Iran but chose to stand by her principles and oppose the regime. She worked as a consultant, offering legal advice, writing articles, and speaking out in public about the rights of the most vulnerable in Iranian society—women, children, dissidents, and minorities—and pushing for legal change. In 2003, she received the Nobel Peace Prize for her efforts, but this put her under even greater pressure from the Iranian government (she had been closely monitored since the 1990s with phone tapping, death threats, and imprisonment).

Shirin paid a high price for her integrity. Her family, including her two daughters, were put under enormous strain because of her activities; her brother and sister suffered many interrogations; and after she was forced to leave Iran in 2009, her husband was framed, imprisoned, and beaten (they subsequently divorced after thirty-seven years of marriage). She tells her story in her powerful memoir, *Until We are Free: My Fight for Human Rights in Iran*. Her aim in writing it was to show what the people of Iran have had to endure under the police state of the last decade, particularly the many Iranian political prisoners and prisoners of conscience, especially journalists, lawyers, women's rights activists, and students who oppose the regime. Her integrity and courage are hugely to be admired and demonstrate what is possible for a human being to achieve in such circumstances.

I try always to live with integrity.
I am committed to changing the circumstances of my life through changing my attitude.
I am finding the courage to pursue new possibilities.

9. Clarifying our vision

Whatever it is that we hope for in our lives—the basic requirements of health, home, relationships, and a means of livelihood if those things are problematic for us; to overcome some past trauma or hurt and to move on with our lives; or something we long to do but have not so far had the opportunity to try, or we hesitate to attempt—clarifying what we really want for ourselves is vital. We can begin by visualizing what we want in our life, what it might look like, and how we might feel with it in our life, and then imagining the steps to achieving it.

Everything we create in our life starts out as a mental image in our minds, whatever we're doing, whether it's baking a cake or planning a holiday or designing a garden. So we have practical experience of the fact that it's not difficult to harness the natural power of our imagination to create a clear image of how we want our life to be. When we form that mental image, we can then allow it to become the experience so that we really can see and feel ourselves in the situation we want, giving it hopeful, positive energy. It's important to be in as relaxed a state as possible, in day-dreaming mode as it were.

It may be helpful to write down in a specially designated notebook our goal and the steps needed to achieve it. Visions can become reality when we are specific and when we work on visualizing our future—perhaps for five to ten minutes a day, whatever situation we're in. Consistency is important, as is the need for flexibility, so that we can adapt and reposition ourselves should the unexpected happen, as it likely will.

Using actual images is also helpful. It's said that a picture is worth a thousand words, and certainly the subconscious mind does not distinguish between a real or imagined situation. Using images also works because it overrides any negative self-talk that gets in the way of achieving our objective. It's also a way of telling the universe of our wish to manifest something different for the future.

We can collect images from magazines or draw pictures of what we want to create and paste them into our notebook or on a board so that we can use them as reminders. We can place them where we will be able to see them every day, perhaps on our dressing table, our desk, or in the kitchen. We can try to picture ourselves in this future scenario and how it feels. Imagining a timeline is helpful too—"by X, I will have achieved Y," etc. Constantly reviewing and making adjustments to this work in progress is also a good idea.

Gradually, as time passes, identifying our goals and working toward them become a habit. With a new way of life, with a sense of purpose, we begin to feel differently, we begin to behave differently—and things begin to change.

I proclaim to the universe that I am manifesting something magnificent for the future.
I am using my imagination to create a picture of how my new life is unfolding.
I am developing a sense of purpose.

10. Embracing our unique destiny

When we follow our dreams, we're choosing hope over fear. Instead of feeling as though we're staring into an abyss and everything is hopelessly impossible, we dare to believe that things can be better. Our current circumstances can change because we choose to change. We can become commensurate with what life offers us now, seeing the possibilities that are there, and envisioning a future that is more alive and meaningful. Mark Nepo, a poet-author of great insight and understanding, wrote: "Our job is to nourish the spark of life we each carry inside us." Our unique destiny is to live a life that is meaningful and therefore makes us happy.

Victor Frankl, the famous Viennese psychiatrist who survived the Holocaust and wrote about his experiences in a Nazi concentration camp in his best-selling book, *Man's Search for Meaning*, concluded that it was "meaning" that made the difference between those who lived and those who died:

> Everything can be taken from a man but one thing, the last of human freedoms—to choose one's attitude in any given set of circumstances, to choose one's own way.

Creating our vision of the future

Our unique purpose is to find meaning, to understand the value of suffering, and to feel that we are responsible to something greater than ourselves. It is finding this satisfying life purpose that makes us happy rather than pursuing happiness itself. It is the pursuit of meaning that is paramount, which means devoting our lives to giving rather than taking. When we embrace our unique destiny and learn to serve, we exude energy and joy and so become a beacon of hope for others.

Harriet Tubman, a great icon of American freedom, was certainly a beacon of hope for others. Born a slave, she was frequently beaten and suffered a severe head wound that caused her health problems throughout her life. Her faith in God, however, was unshakeable.

In 1849, with hope in her heart and an image of a better life for herself, she had the courage to make a bid for freedom. Not content with that alone, she returned to rescue her family, gradually bringing them all to safety. With an even greater sense of purpose, she then guided dozens of slaves to freedom, traveling at night and on foot—helped by a network of activists—and avoiding the slave catchers. Her trust that God would keep her and those she was helping safe proved valid, for none of them was ever caught. She went on to rescue more than 750 slaves during the American Civil War.

In her later years, Harriet Tubman worked to promote the cause of women's suffrage. She died in 1913 at age ninety, and has inspired generations of black Americans struggling for equality and civil rights.

Her words remind us how important it is to create our meaningful vision of the future:

> Every great dream begins with a dreamer.
> Always remember, you have within you the
> strength, the patience, and the passion to reach
> for the stars to change the world.

I choose to change.
I nourish the spark of life I carry inside myself.
I have everything I need to change my world.

Chapter 2

Having conviction and holding on to our ideals

> *You may encounter many defeats, but you must not be defeated. In fact, it may be necessary to encounter the defeats, so that you can know who you are, what you can rise from, how you can still come out of it.*
> —MAYA ANGELOU

Once we've set our internal compass toward a vision of a better future, there is less chance of us coming unstuck, even if we experience setbacks. We're buoyed up by hope, having faith in our dream, and even the smallest of events seems imbued with possibility. Instead of doubting and being fearful, we're able to use all our ingenuity and imagination to fathom out how to reach our goals. We've made a commitment to this undertaking, and we intend to see it through. As the poet Langston Hughes, the leading voice of the Harlem Renaissance, wrote, "Hold fast to dreams, for if dreams die, life is a broken-winged bird that cannot fly."

According to psychologist Charles R. Snyder, who came up with the "Hope Theory," those of us who have hope have the will and determination to reach our goal, as well as the strategies to get there. Hope enables us to believe that we have the capacity to attain the future we've envisaged.

When the commitment to our vision is total, to the extent that we cannot turn back, we can move forward. When fully committed, we achieve the seemingly impossible because not only does commitment give us the necessary energy and self-belief, but we're also fueled by the unexpected help that always follows as an inevitable result. Goethe, the great German Romantic writer, described this process:

Until one is committed
there is hesitancy, the chance to draw back,
always ineffectiveness.
Concerning all acts of initiation (and creation)
there is one elementary truth

the ignorance of which kills countless ideas
and splendid plans:
That the moment one definitely commits
       oneself
Then Providence moves too.
All sorts of things occur to help one
That would never otherwise have occurred.
A whole stream of events issues from the
       decisions
Raising in one's favor all manner
Of unforeseen incidents and meetings
And material assistance
Which no man could have dreamt
Would come his way.

We can also be inspired by what others have achieved, even against great odds, for it enables us to realize we are not alone in this process of trying to hold on to our ideals. Believing in ourselves, we can value the life we've lived so far that has given us experience and understanding. Knowing that our time on earth is limited, we can focus on our priorities and harness the power of intention. As our awareness develops, the life force can flow through us, and we can more easily access opportunities. While staying grounded, we also keep the faith and hold on to our ideals.

Having conviction and holding on to our ideals

1. Breaking through our resistance and doubt

In spite of our decision to opt for hope and pursue our vision, we may at times find that our old habits of thought and feeling get in the way. When we encounter an unexpected stumbling block, our doubts and fears surface once again and lead us astray. How do we go about breaking through our resistant patterns?

We have to remind ourselves that the choice is ours. We are responsible for our thoughts and our actions, regardless of the circumstances we find ourselves in. Why revert to a way of thinking that has not served us well? Far better to go forward in hope, remembering that life is full of possibilities. Where we are is the result of choices we have made so far. Setbacks are merely the challenges that, as we consider and deal with them, make us stronger and more determined to achieve our goals.

Amelia Earhart, the American pioneer aviator, knew from the moment she first went in a plane in 1920 that she absolutely had to fly. She had emerged from a troubled childhood longing to be a successful woman. Her hospitalization with pneumonia resulted in chronic sinusitis, which later became a significant handicap to her flying. But Amelia was not going to let anything like that hold her back from achieving her dream and becoming "Queen of the Air." She had to work hard at a variety of jobs to save enough money for flying lessons, and she had various sinus operations to try to improve her condition. Undeterred, she went on to make her first solo flight across North America, and she became the first woman to fly solo across the Atlantic Ocean. There must have been occasions when she had her doubts, but she clung tenaciously to her dream. As she so aptly put it, "The most difficult thing is the decision to act, the rest is tenacity."

J. K. Rowling, author of the Harry Potter series of books, conceived the idea for the series while on a delayed train; she also held on to her vision in spite of difficulties. In the seven years that followed her first having the idea, her mother died, her first child was born, she was divorced from her first husband, and she was then living on state benefits as a single parent. We know that it wasn't easy for her because she has been open about feeling a failure. She was diagnosed with clinical depression and even contemplated suicide. She kept going, however, until she finished her first novel. Several rejections didn't make her give up, and within five years she had become the success story that we all know

Having conviction and holding on to our ideals
....

about. Now a multimillionaire, she has a charitable trust with a mission to combat poverty and social inequality.

For each one of us facing doubts—head-on is the only way through them. Letting go of old patterns requires courage, but when we refuse to let fears, doubts, or rejections bring us down, and maintain instead a hopeful and positive attitude, the path forward becomes clearer. Expecting good things to happen while continuing on the path means we are more likely to be able to respond to the good that is all around us.

> *I have the will and determination to reach my goal*
>   *and the strategy to get there.*
> *I am committed to my vision of the future.*
> *I maintain a positive and hopeful attitude and expect*
>   *good things to happen.*

2. Reminding ourselves of the heroism of others

One of the things that can really help us when coming up against setbacks, and perhaps grappling with doubts about achieving our goals, is to look at how others have coped in difficult situations. What kept them going when times were tough? How did they manage to summon up hope even in the most dangerous of circumstances?

Amanda Berry was one of three girls kidnapped and held captive for over a decade in a house in Cleveland. Repeatedly raped, psychologically abused, and threatened with death if she tried to escape, Amanda kept a secret diary that she later drew on to write her book *Hope* (together with Gina Dejesus). In it, she writes of trying to wire her mind to "focus on the hopeful thoughts, push out the negative ones." While in captivity, she gave birth to a daughter, whom she tried to raise as normally as possible given the horrendous conditions of her captivity. She also made a promise to herself that when she was free, she would "live, laugh, love," and remember every moment as a gift. "I am a believer in the power of hope…," she wrote.

The young women escaped in 2013, and in May 2014 they were invited to Washington by the National Center for Missing and Exploited Children, an organization that helped the families of the three girls when they were abducted. They received the Hope Award, which is given every year to someone who inspires hope for missing children.

Having conviction and holding on to our ideals

Although she may never know why what happened to her did happen, there is no doubt that the decade in captivity changed Amanda. She wrote that she was stronger and more aware of the importance of kindness. Above all, because she knows that life can change in seconds, her appreciation of the little things in life has become paramount. Ten years in the life of a young girl is a long time to keep hope alive, but Amanda's story shows what is possible in a seemingly impossible situation. We have a choice, whatever our situation, to choose how we respond, as the Dalai Lama reminds us:

> We can let the circumstances of our lives harden us so that we become increasingly resentful and afraid, or we can let them soften us, and make us kinder.

The women of the Standing Rock Sioux Reservation in North Dakota are heroines who have not given up on hope. Resisting the construction of an oil pipeline that desecrated sacred burial and prayer sites and that threatened the water supply of the surrounding Native American community, these women have never given up hope in spite of being sprayed with tear gas and rubber bullets. Prepared to risk their lives, they have vowed to continue the struggle, believing that their ultimate weapon is prayer, as expressed here in this Pueblo prayer:

Hold on to what is good,
Even if it's a handful of earth.
Hold on to what you believe,
Even if it's a tree that stands by itself.
Hold on to what you must do,
Even if it's a long way from here.

We can empathize with these courageous women who have held on to their ideals, and we can see that our own lives need not be overcome by sorrow and despair. Other women's stories of the challenges they faced and how they held on to hope are an inspiration to us all.

*I know I always have a choice in how I respond
    to life.*
I remind myself that every moment of life is a gift.
I stand firm in my belief in what is good.

3. Believing in ourselves and the value of our experience

Sometimes we doubt that we have the requisite strength and ability to hold on to our vision.

Occasionally, we beat ourselves up because we've fallen short of our ideals in some way or wandered off track, so cultivating self-belief is really important for us all.

We need to remember that we are each unique, with particular gifts we can put to use to achieve our goals. We will be better at some things than others, and it's okay to be gentle with ourselves rather than judgmental if there are some things we find difficult or if we slip up. Each one of us has something special that will serve us well, a talent that we can utilize both for our benefit and for the benefit of others.

When I visited Portland, Oregon, I was intrigued by a beautiful statue of Sacagawea, a Shoshone Indian woman who acted as interpreter on the Lewis and Clark expedition in 1804 to explore the lands beyond the Mississippi. This journey across the Great Plains, the Rocky Mountains, and the western rivers was an extraordinary feat of endurance, during the course of which they encountered subzero temperatures, blizzards, hunger, disease, mosquitos, and grizzly bears!

Captured as a young girl by a raiding party, Sacagawea was enslaved and ultimately purchased by a French fur trader who was hired by Lewis and Clark. Pregnant at the time, and the only woman on the expedition, she was taken along because she spoke Shoshone. Sacagawea proved to be an important asset, not least because she had incredible self-belief and was prepared to voice her opinion about issues such as where they should best spend the winter. Her experience as a Native American woman meant that she was invaluable in being able to search for edible roots and plants and make moccasins and clothing for the party. She has subsequently become an icon of courage for women.

Another inspirational example is Ann Davison, largely unknown these days because she was not as publicity seeking as some are. She was the first woman to sail single-handed across the Atlantic—3,310 miles from Plymouth to Antigua. What is remarkable is that this was her second attempt, her first having been disastrous. She and her husband had a series of financial difficulties, and deeply in debt, they had fled their creditors to avoid having their seventy-foot boat impounded. Beset by gales, their boat eventually smashed up on Portland Bill on the south coast of England. Ann's husband died, while she survived fourteen hours adrift on a life raft and was washed ashore. Few women would have wanted to attempt the crossing again, let alone on their own. Ann pulled her life back together, however, and in memory of her late husband, and also as a personal test of everything that had gone before, she had enough self-belief to achieve her goal some years later.

We too need to believe in ourselves and put our skills to good use. When we value our life experience and are prepared to put it to the test, we flourish and can feel hopeful about the future.

I believe in myself and my abilities.
I am utilizing my talents for myself and others.
My self-belief grows stronger every day.

4. Realizing our time on earth is limited

Hope becomes crucial as we begin to age, and above all, we hope we will be blessed with good health and will achieve a measure of serenity. When we're young, we don't much think about it and assume we will live beyond the biblical three-score years and ten, yet the reality is that we don't know what may befall us, and at any point our life could come to an end.

As children, we can't wait to grow up, yet as time passes, we often wish we were younger, particularly in our youth-obsessed culture. We have to face the fact that energy begins to decline, we start to creak, we face a continuing series of losses, and generally we become frailer with old age, even though we still feel young inside.

Hope lies in having a spiritual perspective, recognizing that we are not merely the physical body, but something else altogether—a divine spark that exists beyond time. This part of us never ages.

Alice Herz-Sommer was sustained by hope and made the best of everything that happened to her during the course of her life. She was Jewish, born in Prague, and became a music teacher. She survived the Theresienstadt concentration camp, playing in concerts, along with other musicians, for the prisoners and guards. She said:

> Music is magic. We performed in the council hall before an audience of 150 old, hopeless, sick and hungry people. They lived for the music. It was like food to them. If they hadn't come (to hear us), they would have died long before. As we would have.

Alice's husband died in Dachau. Her son survived, and after the war, she lived for forty years in Israel, where she taught at the Jerusalem Academy of

Music. In 1986 she moved to London, close to some of her family. She practiced the piano three hours a day until the end of her life at the age of 110.

Alice knew that holding on to hope was vital. In *A Century of Wisdom: Lessons from the Life of Alice Herz-Sommer*, she states:

> I look at the good. When you are relaxed, your body is always relaxed. When you are pessimistic, your body behaves in an unnatural way.
> It is up to us whether we look at the good or the bad.

When we can exist without any anxiety about the future or brooding upon the past, age no longer matters. We live as fully as possible, in the present moment, whatever point we're at on our life's journey.

> *I know that I am much more than my physical body.*
> *I am making the best of everything that happens to me in life.*
> *I am free from anxiety about the future.*

5. Being optimistic yet realistic

Hope is a process that we learn when we have to grapple with difficult circumstances. It's not something passive, but a courageous choice we make. It accepts the pain, yet at the same time realizes there is the possibility of change for the better. As well as a choice, hope is an action that we have to practice until it becomes a habit, for what we practice, we become.

Optimism is not quite the same as hope but is linked with it, and there is evidence that it's inbuilt. Optimism is about seeing the glass half-full rather than half-empty, which on the whole we have a natural tendency toward. It's actually inherent in our survival mechanism, possibly being hardwired by evolution into the human brain. However, both neuroscience and social science suggest we tend to be more optimistic than realistic—the so-called optimism bias; for example, we tend to overestimate how long we will live or how successful we will be, while underestimating our chances of getting divorced or being diagnosed with cancer. The bias helps protect us and inspires us to keep going. Scientific research studies show optimists tend to work longer hours, earn more, and save more; they are more likely to remarry, eat healthier diets, and exercise more. They also show that being optimistic helps make us less anxious, lowers stress levels, and improves physical health. A Harvard study in 2016, looking at more than seventy thousand women between fifty-three and eighty-three, confirmed that there were greater health benefits to optimism, with a lower risk of death from heart disease, stroke, cancer, respiratory disease, and infection.

It seems therefore that, although positive expectations enhance our chances of survival, because we can also be overoptimistic, we need to ensure that we develop our awareness and thus strike a balance with realism. We need in effect to be realistically optimistic so that we maintain the glass is half-full, but at the same time are practical, believing that things will turn out well yet taking precautions and being flexible.

Eleanor Roosevelt, the much admired wife of the President Franklin D. Roosevelt, had a painful childhood and a challenging marriage. This meant she was able to empathize with those who suffered, and she worked tirelessly for women's rights in the second half of her life. In *You Learn by Living*, she writes:

It is not wishful thinking that makes me a hopeful woman.... Surely in the light of history, it is more intelligent to hope rather than to fear, to try rather than not to try. For one thing we know beyond all doubt: Nothing has ever been achieved by the person who says, "it can't be done."

It's far better to have an optimistic attitude toward the challenges we face, rather than be weighed down by disappointment, worry, and self-pity. When we're negative, it does no good at all, sapping our energy and taking away hope. When we think optimistically, our energy increases.

Words have great power, so it's important to talk optimistically rather than complain. Complaining rewires our brain for negativity, so we need to ensure that we trigger our neural network for optimism. We can use affirmations to help us feel optimistic. If we can look for the good in everything; believe the best about people and situations, without being like Pollyanna; and be grateful for what we have, then we will find that each day turns out better for us than if we had given way to negativity.

Our circumstances don't necessarily change immediately, but our hopes and expectations change

Having conviction and holding on to our ideals

us and we react differently to life. This shift in perspective makes all the difference: Realistic optimism carries us through and gives us strength; it heals and brings peace of mind.

> *I practice hope so that it becomes a habit.*
> *I choose to believe that things will turn out well, but I also remain flexible.*
> *I increase my energy by being realistically optimistic, and I look for the good in everything.*

6. Developing our capacity to be aware

Sometimes our thoughts and feelings—and consequent behavior—get in the way of achieving our dreams. We often sabotage ourselves with negative thoughts and attitudes without really realizing it. They have become ingrained habits, stemming from our earliest experiences in childhood, and reinforced over the years by our experience of life.

Fortunately, as human beings, we have the capacity to be self-reflective, and it is this ability that enables us to make choices and empowers us to learn and grow, particularly if we adopt practices that increase our awareness. When we become more aware of the activity of our subconscious mind through paying attention to what's going on inside us, then greater understanding and insight are the result. Neuroscience, biology, and genetics have all demonstrated that when we increase our awareness, we are able to change the negative thinking and bad programming from our past.

One of the best ways of becoming more aware of our automatic reactions, attitudes, and behaviors is to practice mindfulness. This technique is about being as awake and conscious as we can; learning to control our focus of attention; and noticing our thoughts as well as the sights, sounds, and smells around us. From the moment we wake up in the morning, we can try to be in the present moment, reminding ourselves that we are blessed to have another new day ahead of us, full of possibilities. We can endeavor to be conscious of all our normal daily activities—from getting out of bed, stretching, taking a shower, putting on our clothes, brushing our hair, preparing breakfast, and so on throughout the day. Usually, we don't pay that much attention to what we're doing; we're on autopilot and maybe replaying an exchange we had last night or thinking about our schedule for the day. According to one research study, the average person is focused 80 percent of the time on the past

Having conviction and holding on to our ideals

or future. When we are more aware of the present moment, we come to understand ourselves better.

Meditation is an excellent tool for increasing our awareness. It helps us move beyond the analytical mind so that we become conscious of what was unconscious. Over time we learn to observe the thoughts, feelings, and sensations that arise and let them go, rather than getting caught up in them.

There are numerous meditation techniques, but working with the breath or repeating a mantra are probably the simplest to use. Working with the breath at its most basic level is merely to follow the breath as it moves in and out of the nostrils, or to feel the abdomen expanding and contracting with each inhalation and exhalation. A mantra can be any meaningful word or phrase repeated over and over to help calm the mind. Visualization, which we have already looked at (pp. 44–45), involves working with an image, which could be a lake, a mountain, a tree, whatever we feel comfortable with and works for us. We might try contemplative walking, where we place one foot in front of the other, walking slowly and being mindful of every aspect of the movement. Conscious relaxation, where we lie down and focus on each part of the body, telling it to relax, is also very helpful. Loving kindness meditation (see pp.

169–70) is a technique in which we aim to improve our compassion toward ourselves and others.

The key to all meditation is to watch our thoughts arise without being drawn into them, but letting them go. If we can cultivate stillness and peace, observing and trusting the present moment, without labeling or judging, we may perhaps have a sense of the higher energy frequencies and of connecting with something beyond ourselves that we may call God, Nature, the Life Force, the Source, the Self (with a capital *S*), the Atman, the Supreme Reality, Chi, or even the Zero-Energy Field.

Ultimately, when we practice mindfulness and meditation, we accept that we are on a journey and know that we have to be willing to practice every day if we want to make progress. The work is about inner development, about growing and developing our true potential as human beings. As Jon Kabat-Zinn, at the University of Massachusetts Medical School and author of a number of excellent books, put it:

> Meditation is more rightly thought of as a "Way" than as a technique. It is a Way of being, a Way of living, a Way of listening, a Way of walking along the path of life and being in harmony with things as they are.

Having conviction and holding on to our ideals

Meditation and mindfulness practiced over time are scientifically proven to make a difference. They can change our brain, as researchers at Harvard Medical School have found in various experiments. Long-term meditators were found to have the same amount of gray matter as twenty-five-year-olds, despite the cortex shrinking as we age. Using the latest in MRI brain imaging technology, researchers from the University of Wisconsin confirmed that meditation naturally harnesses the brain's neuroplastic potential; that's to say, it increases the strength, size, and density of our brains, and gets the left and right sides of our brain to work in harmony. It has been shown that even practicing for as little as thirty minutes a day for eight weeks can bring about beneficial changes to our brains. There is heightened awareness, enhanced focus and concentration, increased access to intuition, and greater learning ability as well as the health benefits of lowering stress levels, boosting endorphin and serotonin levels, overcoming depression, and eliminating insomnia.

All are good reasons, therefore, to take up the practice of meditation and mindfulness, so that we make better choices at key moments in our lives and ensure happier and more fulfilling futures.

I am changing the negative thinking and bad
   programming from my past.
I practice being awake and conscious.
I am developing my true potential as a human being.

7. Harnessing the power of intention

There is a growing amount of scientific evidence from quantum physics to neuroscience that everything in the universe is interconnected. Indigenous societies have always regarded the universe as an indivisible whole, but for the last few hundred years, society in the West has seen itself as separate from Nature and as something to be controlled by man. Competition rather than cooperation dominates our culture, and we see the detrimental consequences in the crises that seem to be overwhelming our world and the widespread sense of fear and uncertainty that prevail.

If we look at the history of evolution over millions of years and several extinctions, life seems to have evolved by adapting and responding to crises. What seem to have led to adaptation and the ever-increasing complexity and diversity are cooperation, interaction, and mutual dependence.

Having conviction and holding on to our ideals

If all life is interconnected and interdependent— people, animals, plants, etc.—then it's not surprising that our minds can have an effect on everything around us. Intention, which is focused thought, creates reality and has an innate power to change things. There is now a wealth of evidence that supports the idea that our minds, thoughts, and beliefs have an effect—both on us and on our well-being, and on others. Whether it's guided imagery techniques slowing the growth of cancer cells, or athletes mentally practicing their training routine and being able to improve their muscle strength, or prayers for healing that seem to be effective in improving the health of others, or water changing its molecular structure through blessing—we seem to be able to affect and change things.

Our intentions are powerful. When we have the intention to change our lives and fulfill a dream, our brains leap into action. In his best-selling book *Into the Magic Shop: A Neurosurgeon's Quest to Discover the Mysteries of the Brain and the Secrets of the Heart*, James Doty shares his story of changing his life through harnessing the power of intention. As a troubled youngster with an alcoholic father and an invalid mother, he had the good fortune to meet someone who taught him meditation and visualization practice along with self-hypnosis. His perspective was so changed that instead of seeing limited possibilities for himself, he saw instead endless opportunities. He eventually became a neurosurgeon and a successful entrepreneur, but now directs Stanford's Center for Compassion and Altruism Research and Education. Together with his colleagues, he has conducted various research projects that prove that merely thinking about performing an action, seeing, or doing something in our imagination stimulates part of the brain. The ancient yogis, of course, knew how powerful the mind is through experience rather than science. Whether we wish to follow spiritual tradition or scientific experiment, we can all harness the power of intention and use it to bring about positive change in our own lives.

I harness the power of intention to change my life.
I see endless possibilities for the future.
I am living my dream.

8. Tapping into the life force and reaching for the stars

If everything in the universe, including us, is pulsating energy, then we want to be vibrating at the higher frequencies of hope, openness, and love so that we experience the richness of life with all its abundant possibilities. "The same stream of life that runs through the world, runs through my veins," wrote the great Bengali visionary, Rabindranath Tagore. When we consciously connect with the stream of life, we sense the magical, miraculous nature of existence. When we listen and pay attention, help and guidance come from the most unexpected quarters. People seem to appear in our lives at precisely the right moment, or books fall into our hands with just the information we need, or an exciting project materializes just when we're ready for it.

Sometimes we're too distracted or overwhelmed by our thoughts and emotions and lose that connection with the life force. We're closed and don't see with clarity and therefore miss the opportunities before us. If, however, we can remember that the connection is always there, waiting to be utilized when we're ready to tap into it, then life-changing events can occur.

Aarti Thakur lives in Mumbai, and in January 2012, while she was waiting for a train, a man threw acid in her face in a revenge attack orchestrated because she was engaged and therefore not interested in the man's advances. Badly disfigured, Aarti became depressed, and when her fiancé broke off the engagement, she was heartbroken and despaired of ever finding love again.

Eventually, Aarti realized that she didn't want to be called a victim all her life: "If I want to change the situation, I'm the only person who will take charge of it, nobody else can make it happen for me." She began volunteering with an organization that supports acid-attack survivors. Invited to speak about her experience at an event in 2014, she impressed Prashant Pingale with her bravery in speaking about it. He had courageously shielded his sister in a separate but similar attack, sustaining terrible burns. He made up his mind that he wanted to marry Aarti. They became friends, and after a while, Prashant proposed to Aarti. She accepted his proposal, and they are now married.

Miracles happen. When we make a fundamental shift in our perspective and take responsibility for our lives whatever the circumstances, and when we are courageous and hopeful, our world expands, and the seemingly impossible can happen.

Mandy Harvey of St. Cloud, Florida, wanted to do more with her life than give up. She had been singing since the age of four, but when she was eighteen, she lost her hearing due to a connective tissue disorder. She got sick and the nerves deteriorated. She gave up initially but then figured out a way to get back to music—through her feet, feeling the vibrations of sound. Now twenty-nine, she charmed both the judges and the audience of *America's Got Talent* when she sang with her beautiful voice her own composition, "Try."

> *When I take responsibility for my life, I experience abundant possibilities.*
> *I am open to receiving help and guidance.*
> *I know that changing my situation is always up to me.*

9. Grounding ourselves

As well as reaching for the stars in pursuit of our dreams, we need to keep our feet on the ground, firmly rooted like the ancient trees. The mighty English oaks or the great California redwoods, with their branches reaching heavenward while their roots penetrate deep below the earth to support the immense living structure, remind us of what it means to be grounded.

To be as sturdy as these magnificent trees, whether we're experiencing joy or sorrow, gain or loss, is surely something to aim for.

Stretching up to the sky, a tree catches more of the sun's energy, yet at the same time reaches down into the earth to find water and minerals. The greatest of nature's engines of photosynthesis, trees process carbon dioxide from our atmosphere into the oxygen that we breathe so are vital to our well-being. They are also one of the main anchoring systems of almost every ecosystem on the planet.

Many organizations across the world are now working to plant trees and conserve forests, from well-known organizations like Trees for the Future, Trees for Life, or Trees for Cities, to less well-known projects like the Archangel Ancient Tree Archive, which is cloning some of the world's oldest and largest trees and replanting. Planting trees is such a wonderful symbol of hope.

Wangari Maathai risked her life for trees and for the women of Kenya, and was awarded the Nobel Peace Prize in 2004 for her contribution to sustainable development, democracy, and peace. For the women of Kenya, planting "green belts" has been vital to stop soil erosion, provide shade, and create a source of food and firewood. As far

Having conviction and holding on to our ideals

back as 1976, Wangari, while she was serving on the National Council of Women, introduced the idea of community-based tree planting, which empowered the poorer women in rural areas, for they could see how it improved the quality of their lives. The ordinary people of Kenya then became hopeful for change in the country because of the success of the tree-planting initiative (more than 30 million trees were planted). They felt they could take action to challenge the widespread abuse of power and corruption by the government. In time the tree became a symbol for peace and conflict resolution.

Wangari stood up against the oppressive regime of the country, fighting for democratic rights and encouraging women to better themselves. In spite of threats, beatings, and imprisonment, she courageously held on to her ideals, and her brave campaigns had a ripple effect elsewhere in the world.

In Karnataka in South India, Saalumarada Thimmakka is known as the "Mother of Trees." She and her husband were childless, so they planted 384 banyan saplings over several years along four kilometers of the road to their village, using their meager resources, and hauling water to keep them alive, nurturing and caring for them as children. Now 106 in 2018 (her husband died many years ago), she has received various awards in recognition of her efforts and is frequently invited to tree-planting ceremonies all over India.

In 2016 in the state of Uttar Pradesh, 800 thousand Indian activists planted 50 million trees in twenty-four hours! The Indian government has put aside $6.2 billion to plant trees all over India to combat pollution and stop soil erosion.

Trees remind us of the need to be rooted, and when we stand firm, we not only help ourselves but also can be of service to others.

I remain firmly rooted like a great tree.
I hold on to my ideals and stand firm.

10. Keeping the faith

However difficult our predicament, when we have faith, we know that things can change. When everything seems broken, we have to hope that our life, even if it can't be as it was before, can to some measure be healed, and maybe we can live ultimately in a way that is better.

Naomi Levy was in the first class to admit women to study to be a rabbi at the Jewish Theological Seminary of America; she went on to become a rabbi of a congregation in California. Her life was devastated as a fifteen-year-old by the murder of her father in an attempted robbery. The tragedy shattered her belief in God, but over time she was able to find a way through the darkness. The flame of hope became ignited within her, and she found invaluable lessons hidden in her experience of pain.

In *To Begin Again: Rebuilding Your Life After Bad Things Have Happened*, Naomi Levy writes: "We all have the capacity to return to life, to recover our hope and our trust and our faith. We all have the potential to experience joy once more, to face this world with optimism and renewed strength."

All of us lose something in life and are wounded— our youth and innocence, our dreams, a relationship that really mattered, or family and friends—and we suffer as a result. As long as we are alive, however, we cannot give up hope, for that is to give up on the life that has been given us. We have to face the darkness and rejoin the world around us. We need to shed tears and grieve, for sure—but healing takes time. As Naomi reminds us:

> No matter what we have lost in our lives, there is always something that survives to start over with. There is always some shard, some shred of hope, some way to begin again.

Gradually, we learn to keep our hearts open, and as we face the world with hope, our faith in life is restored.

I am discovering the lesson within the pain I am experiencing.
Even if things cannot be as they were before, I know that my life can be healed.

Having conviction and holding on to our ideals

Chapter 3

Daring to take action

Life shrinks or expands according to one's courage.
—Anaïs Nin

We cannot wait for hope to arrive—we have to decide to have it and act accordingly. Hope is a catalyst and gives us the courage to shake off despair and face the unknown. To take those first steps out of our fear zone into a future that we tell ourselves is going to be better than where we are now can be daunting, but daring to act is a brave choice.

When we make that decision to be hopeful, we're energized and can work toward achieving our dream. We're creating a "hope circuit" by building an expectation that we can create a brighter future.

We make decisions and choices that seem right for us and the future we envisage, and we begin to live with the awareness that we are surrounded by possibilities.

As we let go of the ways of thinking that have kept us stuck, we're more able to stand firm and are not put off by the doubts of others or criticism of the way we now see things. We find we can embrace the changes that lie ahead. When we are no longer closed down, but open to life with all its opportunities, miracles begin to manifest, and as we begin to feel more expansive, we may well want to contribute our skills and talents in helping others, giving them hope too. As the writer Zadie Smith put it, "You are never stronger than when you land on the other side of despair."

1. Being willing to step into the unknown

Realistic hope enables us to believe that we can cope with what lies ahead and gives us the courage to step into the unknown. Without being prepared to take a risk, we don't make new discoveries about ourselves or what it means to be a human being, nor can we find the fulfillment and happiness we long for.

The lives of extraordinary women who have broken the conventions of the societies they lived in are always inspiring. Women travelers from earliest times have risen to the challenge of going beyond the limits of everyday endurance, driven to explore the potential of being human and adapting to conditions that are both challenging and dangerous. Marjorie Kempe, born in England in 1373, set out at the age of forty on a pilgrimage to Jerusalem. Aphra Behn, born in 1640, lived in Surinam in her twenties and later became a spy in Antwerp. By the eighteenth century, women travelers who had accompanied their husbands on the Grand Tour and had become widows continued to travel and live unconventionally—for example, Hester Stanhope who made her home in Syria. The nineteenth century produced an extraordinary crop of female travelers, carrying out missionary or humanitarian work, like Mary Kingsley in Africa and Annie Taylor in China and Tibet. Gertrude Bell immersed herself in archaeology and traveled widely in the Middle East. The colorful Alexandra David-Neel traveled in Tibet with a young Sikkimese priest, and the flamboyant Isabelle Eberhardt rode among the warring tribes of the North African Desert.

Daring to take action
....

Many of these women travelers had to deal with fear, discomfort, loneliness, extremes of temperature, hunger and thirst, sleeplessness, and illness; they also had to be courageous enough to face death. Their strongest weapon for survival was their belief in themselves and in their ability to reach their destination.

Nineteenth-century botanical artist Marianne North showed plenty of daring and self-belief for a woman in conventional Victorian society, finding enormous fulfillment in following her passion for plants. Although used to traveling with her wealthy father, after his death she decided that nothing was going to hold her back from exploring the world and painting its flora—in spite of little formal art training. Traveling mostly alone, she didn't dig up specimens and bring them home, like the male naturalists of the day, but chose instead to paint them in their natural habitat.

Ever hopeful of finding the rarest and most exotic plants, Marianne risked terrain of the most challenging kind to find them—in America, Canada, Jamaica, Brazil, Chile, Borneo, Java, Ceylon, India, Australia, New Zealand, Tasmania, and South Africa. She managed to document accurately in oils the plant life she found. She was respected by botanists and scientists and admired by the public. She produced over eight hundred paintings, which can be seen at the Marianne North Gallery in Kew, London.

At another time and in another very different society, sixteenth-century Indian mystic and poet Mirabai found the courage to leave behind her family and caste in pursuit of a life that she believed would be more fulfilling. She was born into a privileged Hindu family, and when she was eighteen, a marriage was arranged for her with a Rajput prince. Since childhood, Mirabai had been devoted to the Hindu god, Lord Krishna. Her refusal to conform to the different Rajput duties and rituals caused outrage among her new family.

After both her husband's and her father's deaths, Mirabai shocked Hindu society by leaving her home to wander and pursue her path of devotion to Lord Krishna. She knew that this was what she wanted above anything else and was prepared to take the risk regardless of the consequences. Her courage and commitment helped revitalize the tradition of devotional yoga in India, and she is now highly regarded, especially among women. Through her poetry, she expressed the longing of her soul for union with Krishna as well as her pain and alienation as a rebellious female in the male-dominated Rajput culture.

Daring to take action
....

Deep down we all have a longing for happiness and fulfillment, but many settle for less and pursue instead what society tells them is the norm. In our society the emphasis tends to be on being successful and on acquiring the material things that the advertising industry tries to persuade us to buy or enjoy to keep the economy going. This can result in a feeling of emptiness, a kind of soul-sickness that manifests in anxiety, depression, and addiction of one sort or another. We need to listen to those intimations that tell us there must be something more to life and be willing to take a chance, to be courageous, and to put our hope into creating a better and brighter future.

I choose to be courageous.
I know that I can cope with what lies ahead.
I listen to the inner promptings of my heart.

2. Choosing to live more consciously

It's so easy to lose ourselves and become overwhelmed by the plethora of distractions that surround us. We forget the power of attention and, without it, live only on the surface of existence, not really appreciating the richness of the moment. There's nothing wrong with enjoying what the external world has to offer, but when we focus only on this, we lose our center and become disconnected from the flow of life that sustains us. We need to remind ourselves of the imperative of being aware.

When we live with conscious awareness, we are awake and present, fully paying attention to the essence of who we are and what our life journey is about. We are then able to realize the goals that matter to us and do not end up frustrated and exhausted. It does, however, take courage to develop our capacity to be aware and want to grow spiritually. We tend to be self-absorbed, thinking the world revolves around us and our needs. We've spent our lives trying to achieve and acquire what we think we want, yet even if we succeed in attaining the object of our desires, emptiness and a sense of hopelessness can still make themselves acutely felt if we address only our physical, mental, and emotional needs.

Somehow we have to let go of the ego and its ever-more-demanding wants. We have to have the courage to recognize that we are all both human and divine and that it's pursuing the spiritual path that will help make us whole and complete. When we live with the awareness of the changing rhythms of our thoughts, feelings, and desires, we are choosing to live more consciously. We get to know ourselves better.

Daring to take action

The American Buddhist nun Pema Chodron calls it "studying ourselves," by which she means examining and learning from our own experience. Meditation helps us discover clarity and honesty. As we gain insight about why we feel the way we feel, we begin to be less self-absorbed and begin to look to the needs of others.

Life is a never-ending effort to keep walking along the path and not getting overwhelmed by the challenges of daily life. As the poet, artist, and writer Mary Anne Radmacher reminds us, "Courage doesn't always roar, sometimes it's the quiet voice at the end of the day whispering *I will try again tomorrow*." If we can constantly try to live more consciously, we will find our lives transformed.

I am awake and present.
I keep walking the path of conscious awareness.

3. Energizing ourselves and standing strong

Once we recognize that the future has the potential to be better, while accepting that things are the way they are at this point in time, then we begin to see ways to improve our lives. By exercising, as it were, our muscles of hopefulness, we have the wherewithal to be strong.

We can be inspired by the lives of others who have chosen to be hopeful and courageous in dark and difficult times. Anne Frank, the young Jewish girl, and her family spent two years in hiding from the Nazis from July 1942 in a secret annex at 263 Prinsengracht in Amsterdam (now the Anne Frank Museum). Those two years were intense, and in her now-famous diary she describes in detail the fear, tensions, hardships, quarrels, depression, and air raids the family experienced. She writes with a maturity beyond her years:

> [T]he war is going to go on despite our quarrels and our longing for freedom and fresh air, so we should try to make the best of our stay here....
> The world will keep on turning without me, and I can't do anything to change events anyway.
> I'll just let matters take their course and concentrate on studying and hope that everything will be all right in the end.

Anne Frank died tragically in Belsen at the age of fifteen. The insight and wisdom revealed in her diary has however proved an inspiration to many who've faced difficulty.

Daring to take action

Somehow we too have to find the hope and motivation to deal with our own challenging situation. Again, Mary Anne Radmacher has wise words for us:

> Speak quietly to yourself and promise there will be better days. Whisper gently to yourself and provide assurance that you really are extending your best effort. Console your bruised and tender spirit with reminders of many other successes. Offer comfort in practical and tangible ways—as if you were encouraging your dearest friend. Recognize that on certain days the greatest grace is that the day is over and you get to close your eyes. Tomorrow comes more brightly....
>
> *I am hopeful and therefore strong.*
> *I am doing the best I can to deal with my situation.*

4. Releasing habits we no longer need

Once we're committed to our vision of a better future, we need to let go of those subconscious fears and beliefs that prevent us from attaining our goal. When we hope for our lives to improve, we need to understand and acknowledge the blocks and obstacles that can sabotage us. These lie hidden in our subconscious minds. We often get stuck in repeating loops of thought, worrying about what happened in the past and becoming anxious about the future.

Over time we can become aware of these subconscious beliefs, most of which were programmed into us between the ages of one and six. They have largely shaped our behavior and the character of our lives. However, because of the neuroplasticity of the brain, they are not fixed and unchangeable. We can rewrite them if we want to. We can let go of the old story we tell ourselves about our lives and the reasons things have turned out the way they have. We have the power to become mistresses of our fate!

Through practices and techniques like hypnotherapy, EFT (Emotional Freedom Technique), CBT (Cognitive Behavioral Therapy), Silva Ultramind System, NLP (Neurolinguistic Programming), and other similar techniques, we can change our brains and thought patterns to create a different story for the future. Hypnotherapy is a complementary therapy that uses hypnosis to treat long-term problems. EFT, sometimes referred to as "psychological acupressure," works by releasing blockages within the body's energy field through a process of tapping on

Daring to take action
....

the end points of the meridians. CBT is a talking therapy that focuses on current problems and seeks to change the way we think and behave in a practical manner. The Silva Method is a mixture of self-hypnosis and meditation and uses the imagination and positive thinking. NLP provides an understanding of how verbal and nonverbal communication affects the human brain and teaches how to excel in both our personal and professional lives. Such techniques have proved to be very effective tools for many to bring about change in their lives, eliminating habits and thought processes that are detrimental in trying to create more fulfilling lives.

> *I release any subconscious beliefs that might prevent*
>   *me from reaching my goal.*
> *I let go of the old story I've told myself about my life.*
> *I am mistress of my own fate.*

5. Using our talents to help others

Part and parcel of this new path of hopefulness is that as things begin to shift for us and our lives begin to change, we find that we want to help give hope to others. We see that we are not alone, we are connected to those around us, and we realize that we feel happier when we do something for someone else who needs help and inspiration. Taking care of our own needs means we are more able to reach out to others. When we do good, we feel good, and what ensues is an upward spiral for everyone around us.

Take the example of the well-known talk-show host, actress, and media proprietor Oprah Winfrey, who has been hugely successful and influential and has donated millions of US dollars to good causes. Hers is a real rags-to-riches story. Born into poverty, the victim of years of sex abuse, she ran away from home at thirteen and was pregnant at fourteen. Through her later work in the media, she became a millionaire by the time she was thirty-two and ultimately became the first black female multibillionaire in history.

Oprah has been an inspiration to millions around the world through her TV shows, books and book club, magazines, and website. She cares and wants to inspire others through her work, using her talent and the understanding that has come from her life experience. She has also been a generous benefactor to others, giving away millions to educational causes and scholarships and to the Smithsonian's National Museum of African American History and Culture.

Daring to take action

Oprah may be a celebrity example of someone who has used her fame, wealth, and skills to benefit others, but thousands of ordinary people volunteer to help the communities they live in, particularly if they themselves have been the recipients of care and support. Dr. Teri Delane started Life Learning Academy to teach troubled kids the skills that empower them to cope with life. She herself had been helped and supported by the Delancey Street Foundation in San Francisco, a well-known self-help program for drug addicts and ex-offenders. Others just want to help build compassionate communities, using the gifts and talents they have. Each one of us, in our own way, can make a difference in the lives of others. We all have the power to spread a little hope and to help make the world a better place for all.

I know that I am not alone but connected to others.
I am taking care of my needs.
I am happy when I offer a helping hand to others.

6. Braving the critics and being defiant

It takes enormous courage to stand up for what we believe in and to speak out. In 1955, Rosa Parks became a legend for her courageous defiance in Montgomery, Alabama. She had grown up with racism and segregation, repeatedly being bullied by white children but fighting back. She had become active in the Civil Rights Movement in 1943 and had already complained frequently about the unfairness of the segregation of blacks and whites on the Mont-gomery buses.

On the evening of December 1, 1955, Rosa Parks refused to surrender her seat on the bus. In her autobiography, *My Story*, she writes that the reason she did this was that she was "tired of giving in":

> I did not want to be mistreated, I did not want to be deprived of a seat that I had paid for. It was just time ... there was an opportunity for me to take a stand to express the way I felt about being treated in that manner. I had not planned to get arrested. I had plenty to do without having to end up in jail. But when I had to face that decision, I didn't hesitate to do so, because I felt that we had endured that too long. The more we gave in, the more we complied with that kind of treatment, the more oppressive it became.

Rosa Parks was arrested, which resulted in the black community boycotting the Montgomery bus company for 381 days. As a consequence, the city repealed its laws. One brave woman courageous enough to say "no" resulted in the beginning of the end of the injustice of segregation.

Equally impressive was the defiance of Malala Yousafzai. At seventeen, she was the youngest person ever to receive the Nobel Peace Prize for her bravery in standing up to the Taliban in her native Pakistan.

Education was an important part of Malala's childhood, but in 2007, as the Taliban began to control the Swat Valley, girls were banned from attending school and prohibited from pursuing cultural activities like dancing and watching TV. By the end of 2008, over four hundred schools had been destroyed by the Taliban.

Malala was prepared to stand up to the Taliban, believing in her basic right to education. She began to blog anonymously on the Urdu language site of the BBC, describing the war in the Swat Valley and how she was forced to stay at home instead of receiving an education. Her voice became louder as she campaigned for her right to go to school.

On October 9, 2012, Malala was shot by the Taliban but was flown to Birmingham in the UK and treated in an intensive care unit. By the following March, she was attending school there.

Malala won the hearts of many around the world, and on her sixteenth birthday in 2013, she spoke movingly at the United Nations in New York. She tells her story in *I Am Malala: The Girl Who Stood Up for Education and Was Shot by the Taliban*.

Together with her father, Malala went on to found the Malala Fund with the specific objective of empowering young girls to achieve their potential through education and to become change agents in their communities. She is now studying philosophy, politics, and economics at the University of Oxford. In March 2018, she returned to Pakistan for the first time, meeting the prime minister. She also inaugurated a school for girls that is being built with aid from the Malala Fund.

These are just two stories of incredibly courageous women who refused to accept the status quo and believed that injustice had to be challenged. Because they were fearless in their defiance, their lives and the lives of many other women changed as a result. We too need to be fearless when we meet injustice so that we can help create a better future for

Daring to take action
....

all. When we are brave enough to take action, the energy of hope sustains us.

> *I am inspired by the bravery of others.*
> *I stand firm for what I believe in.*
> *I am courageous enough to say "no."*

7. Pursuing our path with passion

Hope enables us to become passionate and to pursue our path in a manner that ensures success. When we live with passion, we are able to achieve extraordinary things.

Maxine Ross has had a passion for dancing since the age of seven. By fourteen, she was dancing professionally and has subsequently traveled all over the world performing. The amazing thing is that she's still dancing and teaching dance at ninety. She has taught thousands of students over the years, some of whom have been with her for twenty-five to thirty years! She says that her love of dance is her life and keeps her going; it is her own personal fountain of youth. And at the time I was writing this book, Maxine had no plans to slow down and was still inspiring others.

The composer Ethel Smyth was another wonderful woman with an amazing zest for life. In her essay "What Matters Most in Life," she writes that "doing things by halves is the most boring thing in the world." She believed that you have to throw yourself into life with all your heart and live with passion.

She was a prolific composer of a wide range of music, including chamber music, choral works, instrumental music, and operas, plus orchestral, piano, and vocal pieces, much of which she conducted herself. She also wrote many books, plays, librettos, articles, and essays, particularly after the loss of her hearing, which for a composer must have been a difficult scenario to bear. She had friends among many of the influential figures of the day, from the Pankhursts to Virginia Woolf and George Bernard Shaw. She was also an activist in the women's suffrage movement of the early 1900s and spent two months in Holloway Prison. Typical of Ethel, however, was a story that Sir Thomas Beecham told about visiting her and finding her conducting the women as they marched around the courtyard, singing her anthem composed for the suffrage movement—*March of the Women*.

I am pursuing my path with passion.
I endeavor to live my life so as to be an inspiration
    to others.

Daring to take action

8. Making each moment count

Losing someone to whom we're close always shocks us, particularly if they die young and unexpectedly. Dealing with death and coping with grief are always difficult for us, for those who are left behind always suffer to a greater or lesser degree. If there is a positive hidden in the pain, however, it is the reaffirmation we generally make about living our life to the fullest as a consequence of the loss. Each moment must count because we're reminded that our life too will come to an end and that we do not know when that end will be.

Elizabeth Kübler-Ross, who helped so much in our understanding of the whole issue of death and dying, wrote:

> Death can show us the way, for when we know and understand completely that our time on this earth is limited, and that we have no way of knowing when it will be over, then we must live each day as if it were the only one we had.

American writer, poet, and civil rights activist Maya Angelou certainly made each moment count. Gary Young wrote in the *Guardian* newspaper in 2009:

To know her life story is to simultaneously wonder what on earth you have been doing with your own life and feel glad that you didn't have to go through half the things she has.

Best known for her seven autobiographical works, including the ground-breaking *I Know Why the Caged Bird Sings*, which tells of her life up to the age of seventeen, Maya Angelou had a long and extensive career. Turning her hand to many a varied occupation in her youth, from cook to cabaret performer, she went on to be an actress, director, and producer of plays. She was also active in the civil rights movement, working with Martin Luther King Jr. and Malcolm X. She was honored by universities, literary organizations, and government agencies, and she made many appearances on the lecture circuit until well into her eighties.

A life richly lived is a good thing to aspire to. It doesn't matter how many mistakes we make or what befalls us; it's how we pick ourselves up and shake ourselves off and have the courage to start all over again that matters on our journey through life.

I am living my life to the fullest.
I have the courage to keep starting again.

Daring to take action
....

9. Breaking free and creating
a new story

We don't have to remain trapped by our circumstances. We can leave the past behind and create a new and better story. Sometimes it might seem impossible, but many have learned that the hope of a better life and a can-do attitude change everything.

Chelsea Cameron grew up in a household in Dundee, Scotland. Her parents were addicted to drugs, and there was frequently violence in her home involving drug dealers and other addicts. It's no wonder that Chelsea became a troublesome pupil at Menzieshill High School. However, due to the encouragement of her teachers, who believed in her, Chelsea went on to become head girl, fluent in German, successful in her exams, and subsequently began an apprenticeship in administration. She decided to choose not to let the circumstances she was born into dictate her life, and she hopes to inspire other young people to choose how they want their life to be.

Lydia Higginson was nineteen and living overseas when burglars broke into the house where she was staying and she was sexually assaulted at gunpoint. She reported the assault to the police, but the men were never charged for what they had done to her. She returned to the UK and tried to carry on her life as normal but ended up being diagnosed with anxiety and post-traumatic stress disorder and was unable to cope.

Lydia felt that all her strength, dignity, and sensuality had been taken from her. She realized she needed to do something, so set herself a challenge. She wanted to reclaim her body and so gave away all her clothes and designed and made new ones for herself. Making her own wardrobe made her feel alive as a woman, and through her blog, *Mademywardrobe .com*, women got in touch to share their own stories of pain and healing. Lydia says, "I feel like I have restarted my life, as me, rather than as someone trying to escape myself…. Wearing clothes I have made is the most honest way I have of being in the world." Lydia now runs workshops to teach others how to create the garments they have always dreamed of wearing—clothes are "my art, my therapy, my protection and my connection."

Eva Peron is a dramatic example of someone who refused to be held back by the life she was born into—one of illegitimacy and poverty. She created a new story of mega proportions.

Daring to take action
....

The young Eva Duarte dreamed of becoming an actress and at the age of fifteen ran away to Buenos Aires. Within a decade, she had become a highly paid actress and lived in an exclusive neighborhood in the city. The greatest stage she was to act on, however, was the political one. As the wife of the president of Argentina, Juan Peron, Eva achieved huge popularity because of the way she championed the poor and downtrodden. She came to symbolize the hopes of many for a better life, and by the time she died tragically at the age of thirty-three, she had become a legend.

I refuse to be trapped by the circumstances of my life.
I am creating a new and better story for myself.

10. Manifesting miracles

For all of us, life begins to change as we change, for we no longer see our situation in the same way as we once did. Hope and determination to follow a path that takes us in the opposite direction from despair enables us to see and appreciate the wonder of life and its endless possibilities. Albert Einstein wrote: "There are two ways to live your life. One is as though nothing is a miracle. The other is as though everything is a miracle."

Helen Keller, who has been an inspiration to millions of people all over the world, knew what it was like to be without hope. As an infant, she had become both deaf and blind as a result of an illness (possibly rubella or scarlet fever). She was famous, however, from the age of eight until her death at age eighty-seven in 1968, because she showed the world that miracles can happen and that there are no boundaries to courage and faith.

Helen's disability resulted in her becoming wild and unruly, until her teacher, Anne Mansfield Sullivan, came into her life. Anne worked with Helen with great love and patience, teaching her pupil to both read and write and also to speak. Helen became the first deaf and blind person to receive a degree from Radcliffe College and went on to write her autobiography, *The Story of My Life*, as well as other books, essays, and articles in magazines and newspapers. Having known hopelessness, she was able to write:

Once I knew the depth of where no hope was and darkness lay on the face of things. Then love came and set my soul free.

Helen Keller didn't stop there, however. She became an advocate for women's suffrage, an early member of the American Civil Liberties Union, as well as being a pacifist and a committed socialist. She worked tirelessly for the American Foundation for the Blind for over forty years and was interested in the welfare of the blind wherever they were in the world, traveling extensively to bring hope and encouragement to all.

Helen well understood the need to be courageous, which means taking risks and not trying to avoid danger. "Life is either a daring adventure, or nothing," she famously wrote.

I appreciate the miracle of life and all its wonderful possibilities.
I am inspired to take risks.

Chapter 4

Persevering when it's an uphill struggle

I will persist until I succeed. Always will I take another step. If that is of no avail I will take another, and yet another. In truth, one step at a time is not too difficult. I know that small attempts, repeated, will complete any undertaking.

—Og Mandino

Perseverance may have an old-fashioned ring to it, but it's a useful quality to try to develop in ourselves. Nothing in life is ever straightforward, and if we're to succeed in whatever our goals may be, we have to be determined and move forward, while at the same time maintaining a certain amount of flexibility. To do that through all the challenges we face, we have to be able to hang on to hope.

Sometimes when we're feeling daunted, and hope is in danger of ebbing away, it's easier if we act "as if" we are hopeful. This immediately brings about a shift in our consciousness so that we do actually start to feel hopeful again. It helps too if we actively ensure we take good care of ourselves, nurturing both our bodies—with good nutrition, fresh air, exercise, and restorative sleep—and our minds—with the beauty of nature, music, art, and mindful awareness. When we do this, we find that a sense of balance returns and we begin to feel more positive about what may lie ahead.

We are also stronger to face any difficult emotions that arise and can more easily accept that we are not our feelings. We also see that we have a choice about whether to allow them to remain with us or let them go. We begin to have more confidence in our abilities so that working at what we want to achieve becomes more enjoyable. It's easier to persevere when energy and strength are restored; disappointment and failure can be overcome, and we appreciate that these are the very elements of spiritual growth.

We learn through our journey that we can be resilient and bounce back from disaster and trauma, by making small incremental changes in our lives. We also realize that we can rewrite the story we tell ourselves so that we become the heroine, not the victim. This is true through the very worst that life can throw at us and at the end of our lives too, as playwright and psychologist Florida Scott-Maxwell reminds us:

> Life does not accommodate you; it shatters you. Every seed destroys its container, or else there would be no fruition.

I. Showing up regardless

Sometimes it's hard to maintain our determination. We start out full of hope, enthusiastic, and highly motivated, but then we falter. We fully intend to work toward our goal, but somehow life takes over and our intentions collapse. We come to understand, however, that both perseverance and acceptance of falling short of our goals are part of the process of learning maturity. We have to hang on to the hope that if we show up, things will work out. By the same token, we don't beat ourselves up if we have a temporary lapse in our efforts.

I'm reminded of my own efforts to sing classical Indian raga. I spend time with my beloved teacher, and so great is the joy I feel when I'm singing with her that I feel inspired to practice every day, knowing that if I do, I will certainly be happy and may just become a better singer. Then I'm thrown off course by my routines being interrupted by something unexpected, and my daily practice goes out the window. What I've learned, however, is that whatever is happening, however I feel, however little time seems available, it's better for me in the long run if I show up to play the *tanpura* and practice my scales and compositions.

It's the same with my writing. I may feel stuck all of a sudden and a bit disheartened that it's not going as well as I would like, but rather than allow myself to become depressed about it, I know that the solution is to sit at my desk and write, regardless of how good or bad what I've written seems to be. I may well discard most of what I've produced, but the mere act of showing up and endeavoring to get something written down is vital. I hope that something will come out of it in the end, and another day I will write with ease because I have been disciplined and put in the time and effort. Writer and activist Ann Lamott counsels:

> Hope begins in the dark, the stubborn hope
> that if you just show up and try to do the right

thing, the dawn will come. You wait and watch and work: you don't give up.

This advice also applies to practicing yoga and meditation. When we feel that there's no way we have the time to practice, or we're out of sorts and can't muster the enthusiasm to make that extra bit of effort, that's exactly when we do need to sit on our mat and get practicing. Even for a short period of time, it's worth the effort. We'll soon feel the benefits of becoming more relaxed and having more energy for the tasks we have to tackle.

Every day I show up regardless of what else is going on.
I always feel the benefit of putting in effort.
I gently resume my path if I temporarily lapse in
   my efforts.

2. Not stressing, and acting "as if"

Acting "as if" is a great trick in life that can help us with many of the challenges we face. If we're anxious and become stressed, we make it more difficult for ourselves to achieve our goals and wear ourselves out at the same time. If we act "as if" we feel hopeful, courageous, and determined, then we start to become so. A good way to deal with anxiety when we feel it arising is instead to see it as excitement. We're choosing to change our energy field when we step away from our chaotic thoughts and fears and choosing to access a higher vibrational frequency. When we do this, the imbalance in our energy field shifts, and we become calmer.

Ego can take us on a wild goose chase, for when we're driven by ego consciousness, we don't feel part of the whole and don't take others into account unless it suits us; we feel separate and need to compete so that we feel good for a while, or have more of something for ourselves, until the desire for something else arises. We think we're important and that the role we have and what others think of us validates us.

We have to stop striving to be important. When we tune into a larger universal consciousness by raising our own vibrational field, then we no longer see ourselves as separate, but as connected to everyone as well as to all life on the planet.

There is a Taoist parable about a rainmaker, who was sought out by some desperate villagers who had tried everything to bring rain to their drought-hit fields and were facing the prospect of starvation. They had performed all the religious rites they knew—to no avail. The renowned rainmaker agreed to help, and all he asked for was a quiet little hut, in which he proceeded to lock himself up for three days. On the fourth day the clouds gathered, and the rain arrived. The rainmaker explained to the delighted villagers that when he arrived, he had a sense of disharmony in the village. Things were not in order, and he was therefore not in Tao. When he was back in harmony after three days, Tao was restored, and the rain came naturally.

This is one of psychologist Carl Jung's favorite stories; he saw it as an example of synchronicity, whereby our inner attitude is inseparable from what is taking place outside. If we're stressed, then everything external seems chaotic. When we restore ourselves to being in balance, life flows easier for us.

I choose to step away from my chaotic thoughts and feelings.
Life flows easily for me because I feel balanced.
I am part of the whole and connected to all life.

3. Taking responsibility for our feelings and thoughts

Whatever difficulties we're facing in our lives, no one but ourselves can free us from the discomfort or pain we feel. Rather than trying to avoid or escape how we feel, or wallowing in it and consequently indulging in inappropriate behavior, we need to acknowledge our feelings. We ignore them by repressing or denying them at our peril. We have to remind ourselves at the same time, even though we acknowledge them, that we are not our feelings. We exist beyond them and can take responsibility for them.

We always have a choice about whether to continue to be sad, distraught, angry, whatever—or to face the feelings, acknowledge them, and then let them go. If we persist in allowing them to overwhelm us, we will only feel more of the same. By bringing awareness to the feelings, we give ourselves the option of replacing them with hope.

We also have to take responsibility for our thoughts. How we choose to think about our situation is under our control. If we keep thinking about how impossible everything is or how unfair life is, our negative thinking results only in more negative emotions and may well, because of how we end up behaving, attract yet more unpleasant events into our lives that make us unhappy.

If instead we choose hope and try to stay consciously aware and in the present moment, not constantly replaying the events of the past and not stressing about the future over which we have no real control, apart from over our minds, then we can feel more at ease.

As we come to recognize the feelings we are able to accept and release, then there is greater clarity. We are able to understand what contributes to the suffering in our lives, and what produces balance and peace of mind. We don't need to let the losses and disappointments make us unhappy but can try to find some good in our lives.

I discovered this for myself when my life was blown apart by the shock of my husband deceiving me in a fairly horrendous manner and leaving me for the relationship he had embarked on during our marriage. I was devastated, and the pain was literally gut wrenching. For a while I kept playing and replaying the tape-loops of what had happened in my head, angry and hating him more and more—constantly causing myself yet more pain. It was like an open wound that would not heal.

Eventually I saw that I had to face the fact that the situation could not be changed. He was not going to return; the marriage was well and truly over. I felt a failure and an overwhelming sense of disappointment, but I did not want to feel that way for the rest of my life. I had to move on and start a new life.

Persevering when it's an uphill struggle

As I saw this more clearly, I began to make plans for myself, I tried new things, and I discovered that I was stronger than I realized. I could survive, I could have a different life, and that life was entirely up to me.

Many of us have been through this, with divorce or broken relationships of one kind or another. Unless we want to stay trapped in bitterness and wanting revenge, we all move on, having learned more about ourselves and our ability to choose something better for the future.

> *I acknowledge my feelings and recognize that they are not who I am.*
> *I always have a choice about how I feel and what I think.*

4. Dealing with disappointment and failure

None of us escapes disappointment in life, and many of us experience a sense of failure. We have to refuse to let such feelings overwhelm us and try again. I love the lines from Samuel Beckett: "Ever tried. Ever failed. No matter. Try again. Fail again. Fail better." Maintaining our sense of hope is imperative, whatever the battles we have to endure. One thing we can be sure of—perseverance always brings rewards.

Madonna Buder is a Roman Catholic nun, also known as the "Iron Nun." Born in 1930 in St. Louis, Missouri, she entered a convent at the age of twenty-three. In 1970, she joined thirty-eight other nuns to establish a new and nontraditional community, the Sisters for Christian Community, independent of the authority of the Roman Catholic Church, with the freedom to choose her own ministry and lifestyle.

In her autobiography, *The Grace to Race: The Wisdom and Inspiration of the 80-Year-Old World Champion Triathlete Known as the Iron Nun*, she talks of the only failure as being the one of not trying. At the age of forty-eight, she began training for triathlons and completed her first at fifty-two, and her first Ironman event at fifty-five. She became the overall Ironman world record holder in age, at eighty-two, by finishing the Subaru Ironman Canada event in 2012. Her achievements have been amazing, but her success has not been without its trials and tribulations. Setbacks are not failures, she maintains, and whenever she had one, she invariably went on to try again. To Sister Madonna, age is a mind-set. Maintaining perseverance and patience, one mile at a time, is the way to win through. Sister Madonna might well have been

Persevering when it's an uphill struggle
....

influenced by these words of writer and abolitionist Harriet Beecher Stowe:

> When you get into a tight place and everything goes against you, till it seems as though you could not hang on a minute longer, never give up then, for that is just the place and time that the tide will turn.

Diana Nyad is another inspirational example of determination, courage, and perseverance in spite of failure. She was only twenty-eight when she first tried to swim the 110 miles between Havana, Cuba, and the coast of Florida. It was not until she was sixty-four that she achieved her dream, however. "You can live out your dreams," she writes in her autobiography, *Find a Way: One Untamed and Courageous Life*, "if you refuse to ever, ever give up."

Diana had kept herself super-fit for thirty years between her first attempt and when she first tried again in 2011. As a broadcaster and journalist, she had traveled the world during that time, but after the breakdown of her long-term relationship, she had a sense of regret and something missing in her life, which led to a period of soul searching.

She decided to live her wild dream and give the Cuba–Florida crossing another try in her sixties. After intensive training, she attempted it again in 2011. Although she failed four times and experienced unpredictable currents and cross-currents, deadly sharks and box jellyfish, third-degree burns from the ocean salt and chafing during the course of all this, she refused to be beaten. She completed the crossing after two days and two nights of continuous swimming.

Diana believes that difficult and traumatic experiences have their uses, helping us become stronger and learning to put a positive perspective even on the most awful setbacks. "I learned through my own life's journey that one makes oneself a champion and all the other things one becomes."

> *I maintain my sense of hope, regardless of setbacks.*
> *I refuse to give up on my dreams.*
> *I become stronger through my experience of continually trying.*

5. Knowing the value of enduring effort

With hope, we find energy, and with commitment, we get help from unexpected quarters, which is such a welcome bonus because perseverance can sometimes seem like pushing a boulder uphill. We also need to work on developing confidence in ourselves and our abilities, trusting that we will be able to achieve what we aspire to.

Marie Curie, a legend among female scientists, wrote:

> Life is not easy for any of us. But what of that? We must have perseverance and, above all, confidence in ourselves. We must believe that we are gifted for something, and that this thing, at whatever cost, must be attained.

Marie Curie's life was a challenging one, but she was exemplary in her ability to keep on going regardless of difficulties. She knew both deprivation and depression, and experienced sexual discrimination and jealousy from her colleagues. It's extraordinary how she was able to sustain herself through really difficult times with her courage and conviction. She toiled endlessly in her systematic study of physics and chemistry and in her pioneering research to isolate radium. She battled constantly for adequate funding and for recognition. She never really benefitted financially from the discovery that she and her husband Pierre made, and which was to become so important for the world in the future, although she was ultimately awarded the Nobel Prize twice. Having lived a life of sacrifice and dedication, and ultimately triumph, Marie Curie seems never to have wavered in her herculean effort.

I am confident in myself and my abilities.
I know that I can achieve what I want to do.

6. Being tenacious when adversity strikes

Whatever happens in our personal lives or in the world around us, we have to be tenacious in holding on to hope. The much-loved teacher and inspirational writer Wayne Dyer put it graphically:

I suggest that you become like a pit bull holding on to a bone called hope. Keep a death grip on that bone called hope regardless of what comes along, and regardless of the obstacles and so-called failures that have previously induced despair.

Artemisia Gentileschi was able to deal with adversity and went on to become the most important female painter of the Italian Baroque. One of her most famous paintings is a visceral portrayal of the biblical story of Judith slaying Assyrian general Holofernes. In the large canvas, the almost life-sized Judith is depicted as a powerful and determined woman. She has the physical and emotional strength to decapitate the general with his own sword, thus saving the besieged town from his army. Artemisia wrote to one of her clients at the time: "I shall show what a woman is capable of. You will find Caesar's courage in the soul of a woman."

Artemisia had tenaciously held on to her vision of becoming an artist, regardless of the storm unleashed following the notorious rape trial that she was at the center of in seventeenth-century Rome. Her father, Orazio, was a successful painter, and Artemisia trained with him in his studio. He asked his friend, Agostino Tassi, to give Artemisia some lessons in drawing, but Agostino ended up raping the eighteen-year-old on more than one occasion and then refused to marry her. When her father found out, Agostino was arrested. The trial was humiliating for her, since she was accused of not being a virgin and of having many lovers. She even had to endure the indignity of being examined by midwives. The upshot of the trial was that Agostino served only a short term in prison, and Artemisia was married off to a family friend.

Undaunted by what had befallen her, Artemisia rejected the conventional lifestyle and left her husband, determined to continue with her career as an artist. *Judith Beheading Holofernes* seems to have been a cathartic painting for her, possibly expressive of how she felt about the whole Tassi affair. Her tenacity paid off, and she went on to gain the patronage of Grand Duke Cosimo Medici in Florence.

> *I keep the flame of hope alive whatever challenges I face.*
> *I am tenacious in my determination to win.*

7. Staying strong when the odds are against us

Sometimes in life we're challenged to such an extent that we're not sure we can find the strength to continue. Usually we do, however, finding resources we didn't know we had. Most of us, when we look back on a difficult experience, find that we've learned a great deal about ourselves, even though it may have left its scars, and our confidence in coping with adversity in the future grows. If we can adopt a hopeful and positive attitude when the odds are stacked

against us, then we can move through the circumstances more easily.

Rose Kennedy, the matriarch of the Kennedy
family, survived crisis after crisis but refused to suc-
cumb to despair:

> Early in life, I decided that I would not be
> overcome by events. My philosophy has been
> that regardless of circumstances, I shall not be
> vanquished but will try to be happy. Life is not
> easy for any of us. But it is a continual chal-
> lenge, and it is up to us to be cheerful—and to
> be strong, so that those who depend on us may
> draw strength from our example.

Devoted to her family, Rose was an effective
campaigner and dedicated fund-raiser for good
causes. She lost two children in the 1940s, and one
daughter was institutionalized because of the sever-
ity of her mental disability. Her husband, Jack (the
subject of much speculation over his questionable
business dealings and possible philandering), had a
debilitating stroke in 1961, dying a few years later.
Her son John, then US president, was assassinated in
1963, and her son Robert, a senator and Democratic
presidential contender, was assassinated in 1968. Her
youngest son, Edward, a senator, was involved in a

notorious car accident on Chappaquiddick Island, Massachusetts, which destroyed his bid for the US presidency.

Throughout all these misfortunes, Rose Kennedy's Roman Catholic faith sustained her. She continued to hope that life would be worth living and had the grit to continue, facing the public with courage and dignity.

Irina Ratushinskaya was sustained by her Christian faith too. She was a dissident Russian poet and human rights activist who survived appalling torture and abuse in a tough labor camp for women in Mordovia, southeast of Moscow. She served four years of her seven-year sentence for anti-Soviet activity before being released in 1986. Her memoir, *Grey Is the Color of Hope*, written after her release and exile, reveals her courage and integrity. Defiantly she had continued to write poetry on bars of soap while in the *gulag*, memorizing the words of her poems before washing them away. Even in her darkest hours, Irina was determined to live and survive and carry on with what gave her life meaning.

I adopt a hopeful and positive attitude when the odds are stacked against me.

I am confident about my ability to cope with misfortune.

Persevering when it's an uphill struggle

8. Learning resilience to bounce back from grief

All of us will experience grief at some point in our lives. "Suicide grief" is a particularly difficult one to deal with, for not only is there the loss of a person dear to us, but for those who grieve there is also a sense of fear, guilt, and inadequacy.

Cadi lost her partner of several years to suicide in February 2014. Stunned by grief, Cadi struggled in the aftermath of the experience to cope with these feelings. She wrote openly on her blog about her anxiety and being afraid that something bad might happen to her too. She shared her doubts about ever having another relationship and whether she might be incapable of making someone else happy.

Rather than let this feeling spiral into despair, Cadi decided instead to choose hope and to make changes so that she could make more of life. Making big changes can be difficult, but small incremental changes can be powerful, helping us build resilience and gradually drop what stops us from becoming our best selves. Cadi admits that in her case she was lucky to have a supportive family and network of friends; plus she felt able to give up a good job to work part time. Initially, she joined a gym but subsequently preferred being out of doors, so she has become a fair-weather cyclist and an all-weather runner. In the course of training for various events, she has met all sorts of different people, and her life has opened up considerably.

Cadi knows she is stronger as a result of what she's been through. She's developed the resilience to bounce back and create a new life for herself. Having always loved adventure (I met Cadi on a trip to Nepal and Tibet in 2015), she has made that a priority—hence her blog, *An Adventurous Girl*. She believes that time is precious and it's important to enjoy life now.

In 2016, Cadi told her story at a conference on mental health and suicide. She realized then how valuable it can be to talk and share our experience. Losing her partner made her realize the value in everyone's lives: "I want to hear about people. I want to listen and hear their sorrows and happiness." Cadi feels she is a better person because of what she went though. She has grown stronger and more resilient, and as a result, she feels she wants to help others who may have had a similar experience.

Grief is a natural reaction when we lose someone, and it takes time to process that grief. Talking about it and having support are vital. Grief has to be faced, as Prince Harry has admitted very publicly. He refused to think about the death of his mother, Princess Diana, all through his teenage years and twenties, which had disastrous repercussions on his life. He eventually sought counseling support and is now able to talk about his feelings, and he is committed to helping raise awareness of the importance of doing so.

Talking about grief is never easy, but with love and support, we come to recognize that there is hope beyond the other side of grief.

> *I choose hope at all times.*
> *I can face my grief and talk to others about it.*
> *I am stronger because of what I have experienced.*

9. Becoming the heroine of our own life

Feeling ourselves a victim is never a good choice to make when confronted with difficult circumstances. Self-pity, complaining, and pessimism do not serve us well, but take us in a downward spiral increasing our unhappiness and making the situation worse. It's far better to choose to be hopeful that we can get through this, and that when we do, the future will be brighter. We can also ask the universe, the life force, God (whatever term feels most appropriate) to give us strength, courage, and the imagination to change things if we can, and if we can't, then to change the way we think about the circumstances. We can trust that help is available to us, as so many others have demonstrated in their own lives, and that we can become heroines instead of victims. As Oprah Winfrey put it, "Step out of the history that is holding you back. Step into the new story you are willing to create."

Xiaolu Guo is someone who created a new story for herself. With enormous determination and energy, in spite of the most terrible beginning in life, she achieved her goals. She shares her remarkable story in her memoir, *Once Upon a Time in the East*. Xiaolu refused to give in to despair and thus became the self-made heroine of her own story.

Xiaolu's parents gave her away soon after birth to a poor, childless couple. Two years later, struggling to feed her, the couple passed Xiaolu on to her illiterate grandparents, who lived in a primitive fishing village on the East China coast. Surviving on a meager diet, she became fond of her kind grandmother. Sadly, her grandfather was a depressive, beat her grandmother, and eventually committed suicide.

Persevering when it's an uphill struggle
....

During her childhood, her grandmother took Xiaolu to see an old Taoist monk. He told her that she was "a peasant warrior" and that "she will cross the sea and travel to the Nine Continents," something that Xiaolu never forgot.

One day on the shore, Xiaolu met a group of art students painting the scene before them—a sunless, gray sea. She watched as one of the students painted a shimmering blue sea and a burning sunset. Suddenly, Xiaolu saw the possibility of reshaping a drab and colorless world through the power of imagination.

When she was seven, Xiaolu's parents reappeared and took her to live with them in a newly built communist compound with other families. Her father was a government artist working on propaganda paintings; her mother, a former Red Guard, worked in a silk factory by day and performed revolutionary opera in the evenings. Xiaolu's catalog of woes continued through her teenage years—cruelty from her mother (who regarded her as "a food bucket" and "a useless girl"), sexual abuse and violence, and pregnancy at fourteen and an abortion.

Xiaolu was sustained by literature and especially poetry. Her imagination stirred by Whitman and other American poets whom she read in translation, she began to write her own poetry and essays. She dreamed of a better life and was patiently dedicated to her studies, so that when she was eighteen, she was thrilled to win a place to study film in Beijing. Later she became a filmmaker, but her films were blocked in China, so she ended up writing telenovela scripts to survive and also wrote books.

At age thirty, Xiaolu became an immigrant in London and began to learn and write in English. Over the next decade, her English novels were short-listed for prizes, and she directed several award-winning films, including *She, A Chinese.*

Given her unpropitious start in life, it's remarkable that Xiaolu even survived. That she should have had such a degree of hope and self-belief and the determination to create a life for herself, and be able to share her astonishing story so eloquently in a language not her own, is nothing short of miraculous. Toward the end of her memoir, she writes:

> The protagonists of my favourite books were all orphans. They were parentless, self-made heroes. They had to create themselves since they had come from nothing and no inheritance. In my own way I too was self-made.

Persevering when it's an uphill struggle
....

Such a story of courage and endurance against all odds is an inspiration to us all, showing what it's possible to achieve with hope in our hearts, an imagination to envision a different future, and perseverance to make it happen.

> *I ask for strength, courage, and the imagination to change things, and expect to receive it.*
> *I can deal with this challenge, and the future is looking brighter.*
> *I am willing to create a new story for myself.*

10. Never, never giving up

None of us knows what may be just around the corner. Life's unpredictability is something we know in our hearts but tend not to think about too much, which in many ways is a good thing so long as we are not surprised when caught off guard.

Kate Allatt was a working mother with three children; she was also a seventy-mile-a-week fell runner. She was planning to climb Kilimanjaro for her fortieth birthday but instead found herself, following a stroke, with locked-in syndrome, unable to communicate. Doctors said she would never walk or talk again. Five months of her life were then spent "all trussed up like a turkey with wires and tubes everywhere," in fear and frustration, unable to move anything beyond a single eyelid.

With great perseverance, three close friends were able to achieve a breakthrough, using a standard sheet of paper with the letters A–Z and Kate moving her eyelid to indicate the letters of the word she wished to communicate. Kate began to be more hopeful as she was able to communicate. Her biggest challenge was the low expectations of many of the medical professionals, but Kate was determined that she would recover. Instead of going into a care home, she went to the gym and worked intensively with a physiotherapist. Within six weeks, she had progressed from a wheelchair to walking sticks, and within another six weeks, she was able to manage without them.

Kate chose to focus on the goal of being able to run again by the first anniversary of the stroke. The result is on YouTube for all to see—a joyous "shuffle," as she describes it. She now walks her two dogs for a couple of hours every day and makes her living as a motivational speaker. She tells her story in *Running Free: Breaking Out from Locked-In Syndrome.*

Others too have had to contend with locked-in syndrome. The most well-known example

Persevering when it's an uphill struggle

is Jean-Dominique Bauby, whose best-selling memoir, *The Diving Bell and the Butterfly*, was made into a film. Completely paralyzed and unable to speak, Jean-Dominique blinked out the text of his book letter by letter. It is a testament to memory, imagination, and the bravery of the human spirit, and for all of us is a profound message of hope.

Editor-in-chief of French magazine *Elle* and the father of two young children, Jean-Dominique used his imagination to escape his locked-in condition. Shunning despair, he created a life for himself— traveling to exotic places, serving himself delectable meals, sharing his love of music, and describing the things he missed—his family and former lifestyle. Never losing his sense of humor, he never saw himself as a victim or became bitter about the blow fate had dealt him.

Such stories remind us of how important it is to store up happy memories that we can revisit, to commit poetry and music to memory, to be able to use our imaginations to see the beauty of nature in our mind's eye, and to enjoy what delights the senses. We never know whether we will suffer a misfortune like Kate's or Jean-Dominique's that leaves us unable to enjoy life in the manner we once did. Whether it's an illness or disability, captivity of some kind, or as we near the end of life, what we have stored up becomes the food that nourishes our souls and helps sustain us.

I trust that I am able to cope with misfortune.
I always choose hope.
I nurture my soul with happy memories and beauty.

Persevering when it's an uphill struggle

Chapter 5

Cultivating patience

Patience is not simply the ability to wait—it's how we behave while we're waiting.

—JOYCE MEYER

We have all been wounded by painful experiences in life, and providing we're not so paralyzed by loss of hope that we can't accept what has happened, we begin to see the necessity of waiting patiently for things to shift. "Hope is patience with the lamp lit," wrote the early Christian writer Tertullian. As we take one day at a time, hoping that the future can be brighter, we are already moving on toward that brighter future, which does indeed materialize although not necessarily in a manner we could have foreseen.

The root of the word *patience* comes from the Latin root *pati*—to suffer, bear, or tolerate. Being born into this world means we are bound to have to deal with pain and suffering, but if we can learn to be patient and trust that things can change, we are more likely to be able to bear what life throws at us.

In our youth we tend to be impetuous and impatient, but experience teaches us that anything worthwhile—whether it's developing good relationships, building a business, raising children, or improving a particular skill we have—takes time. Life also teaches us that when we're patient, things change anyway and we change too as life moves on.

Healing takes time, whether it's a physical illness or injury, or whether it's an emotional wound or nervous condition—the process of healing cannot be hurried. Waiting can seem endless, but we have a choice about accepting events that are beyond our control. We can rail against them, or we can accept what is. Hope helps, but it's no guarantee that our illness will necessarily be cured, that our loved one will return, that our bipolar disorder will not manifest again, or that we will always get exactly what we so desperately wanted in the shape and form we hoped for it.

While we wait and learn to accept that things are the way they are as cheerfully as we can manage, we discover ways to improve our lives. This doesn't mean that life necessarily gets any easier, but we may begin to feel more commensurate with what life is asking of us. We come to understand that it is unfolding in a manner that helps our growth and development. We begin to realize that patience has real benefits.

If we can stay aware and be receptive through our experience of learning to be patient, we find that our capacity for joy becomes greater. Like the potter hollowing out clay to make a pot, and then hammering it into shape and allowing it to harden in the sun so that it can become a container for refreshing water or wine, so patience carves into our souls so that we can make sense of our experience and feel gratitude for what we have learned.

1. Being prepared to wait

Instant gratification seems to have become the norm: we want something, and we want it now. Consumer advertising urges us, "You deserve it. Why wait? Buy it now!" In the past we saved up to buy something we wanted and went to a store. There was such pleasure in looking at everything, feeling the texture, trying it out before making a purchase. Now we buy almost without thinking about it, instantly with the click of a button and a transaction with a credit card, and almost immediate delivery to our homes. It's the same with cooking: We order takeout or pick up a ready-made meal to put in the microwave because we don't have or want to take the time to cook something from scratch ourselves, and in the process we miss part of the pleasure of eating—the anticipation and reward.

Our attitude to time is usually one of panic at it going so fast. To be busy and have a full schedule is almost a badge of honor. Our social capital is supposedly enhanced by how many engagements we have on our calendar and how busy we are. Deep down we know we need stillness and rest however, and our frayed nerves and exhaustion testify to this need.

We're also impatient to get places. Delays on the road, on trains, or at airports frustrate us, yet in the past, journey times were far slower and there was pleasure in traveling.

Technology has also added to our impatience. Because we're constantly connected to our devices, there's evidence from the telecom companies that the smartphone generation expects content in the blink of an eye. Even a two-second delay in downloading can cause stress and irritation.

Often when we feel we're being inconvenienced by delay, it's an opportunity to slow down and look around us, taking in what's going on and perhaps connecting with other people. Or we can just breathe deeply, close our eyes, and go inward and find some calm and rest. When we are prepared to wait and use time in a way that reconnects us to the stream of life, then the benefit to mind and body can really be felt. By contrast, if we let ourselves get wound up by becoming impatient and stressed, we deprive ourselves of the joy of living and being in the moment. "Adopt the pace of nature: her secret is patience," wrote Ralph Waldo Emerson, the American Transcendentalist poet, philosopher, and essayist.

As a gardener, I know only too well how important patience is. I plant my seeds, bulbs, and perennials in hope but have to wait through the long dark days of winter when they are below the surface of the ground. It seems as if nothing is happening, yet seeds are cracking open, bulbs are putting forth their roots, and perennials are merely resting, gathering their resources and getting ready to grow toward the light. With the warmth and rain of springtime, awakening from the dark, they send up their lush green shoots. We can't hurry them. They will take the length of time it takes to grow and come to fruition. Patiently, I tend and nurture them, enjoying the daily progress that they make as they grow and come into flower.

I delight in slowing down and being still.
I am connected to the stream of life and remain calm.
I am prepared to wait, living in the present moment.

2. Accepting that we cannot control events

Many of us have built our lives to some extent around being in control. We believe that we can protect ourselves in some way, consciously or unconsciously, from real or perceived danger. We crave certainty and security. Whether it's our family, our home, our possessions, our career, our reputation—all these things we call "ours," including our own body—in the end they are subject to change of one sort or another. We may think we have a measure of control, but in reality it's an illusion because we live in an insecure world and we face an uncertain future.

The problem in all this is that we become too self-absorbed, too attached, and too addicted to everything being controlled and perfect. For the same reason, we feel driven to accomplish, achieve, and acquire. We're more concerned about what's on our list of things to do, which gives us a sense of control, than relating to those around us and the beauty of life.

I know from my own experience earlier in life with a full-on career. I took on too much and was running so fast that everything became a blur. I ran myself ragged by trying to be in control. When I try to recall now all that happened and people I knew then, I find it hard to remember with any real clarity some of the specifics. It's just a blur. I recognize that I wasn't fully living then and missed the essence of the experiences I was going through. I paid a price for believing that I was superwoman and ultimately was forced by circumstances to live my life differently.

When something seems so important that we're driven to try to control everything, we need to switch our focus and learn to surrender. Surrender is the only answer to inevitable change. It's only when we let go that we can be receptive to life. This frees us to live in the present when anything and every-thing is possible. There's no need to control the present moment—it just is. If we're not living in the now, it's because we're fretting about the future, or worrying why we didn't control the past better, blaming ourselves or someone else for the way things turned out.

Surrender doesn't mean we're giving up on life or failing in some way, or are defeated or resigned to something. Rather, it means accepting the cycles of life as they are. Spiritual teacher Eckhart Tolle wrote:

> Surrender is the simple but profound wisdom of yielding to, rather than opposing the flow of life. The only place where you can experience the flow of life is now, so to surrender is to accept the present moment unconditionally and without reservation.

The process of surrender changes us. When we live in the present moment, we have more choices and can allow the magic and beauty of life to unfold. We have less fear, we're no longer creatures of habit, we feel less isolated, and we're more open and hopeful about life's possibilities. Our attitude to family and friends is kinder, and we are grateful for the joy we feel and are more aware of our neighbors, our community, and our environment. We're no longer trying to control events, and things don't have to be perfect. They are as they are.

> *I am learning to surrender instead of trying to control.*
> *I yield to the flow of life.*
> *I accept the present moment unconditionally.*

3. Allowing time for the healing process

Hope is vital in the healing process. Long ago Hippocrates, the father of medicine, argued that the greatest force in recovering from illness was the natural healing process of the body itself. He suggested medical students pay attention to a patient's emotions as both a contributing cause in disease and as a factor in healing.

Positive psychology, as pioneered by Martin Seligman at the University of Pennsylvania Positive Psychology Center, has in recent decades borne this out. A wealth of research has demonstrated that a positive mental attitude helps in the overall healing process. Seligman points out that most of positive psychology is for all of us:

[T]roubled or untroubled, privileged or in privation, suffering or carefree. The pleasures of a good conversation, the strength of gratitude, the benefits of kindness or wisdom or spirituality or humility, the search for meaning and the antidote to "fidgeting until we die" are the birthrights of us all.

Laughter too has been shown to be beneficial in healing. Norman Cousins is well known as the man who laughed his way back to health and life, and for his pioneering account of overcoming ankylosing spondylitis, a rare disease of the connective tissue—*Anatomy of an Illness*. In 1964, he was given a few months to live but refused to accept this diagnosis and checked out of the hospital and the medication prescribed. Instead, he took large doses of vitamin C and watched Marx Brothers films and *Candid Camera* shows, laughing until it hurt.

Laughter releases endorphins and so helps ease pain, plus stimulates the immune system to fight disease. A great believer in hope, Cousins wrote: "The capacity for hope is the most significant fact of life. It provides human beings with a sense of destination and the energy to get started." He lived until 1990, many years after his illness was diagnosed.

While Cousins succeeded in extending his life dramatically, healing isn't necessarily always about being cured. We may not recover from a life-threatening illness, but we may become more whole, finding a way to resolve issues that trouble us. The origin of the word *heal* is from the Old English root *hal*, to make whole, to bring together—in other words, to restore harmony and balance. When we feel in harmony, we feel whole. *Health, healing*, and *holy* are all linked to wholeness. It may well be that illness causes us to make changes to the way we live. These changes may enable us to achieve a better balance between the physical, emotional, mental, and spiritual dimensions of our lives so that we find a greater sense of peace. Marc Ian Barasch, writer, environmentalist, and advocate for the inclusion of spirituality into the medical system, described healing as in essence "a process of transformation—from illness to wellness, from dysfunction to integration, from breakdown to wholeness."

This transformation is just as true for emotional healing as it is for physical healing. Resolution takes time. Sometimes emotional pain is so debilitating that our ability to cope and see light at the end of the tunnel is really challenged. When extreme, it can result in serious illness or in thoughts of life not being worth living. The painful emotions have to be worked through, and in the case of severe trauma, with the help of counseling.

For the rest of us, time is the great healer. We realize that getting back into balance is vital, and we become more hopeful for the future. We can help ourselves by imagining our minds like a deep lake, undisturbed by the waves or ripples on the surface, and everything calm beneath the surface.

> *I am becoming more whole by restoring harmony and balance.*
> *I am hopeful, and my mind is calm.*

4. Being receptive to the voice within

Our world today is so full of distractions and noise that silence is a rarity. Because we're stimulated by all that is on offer in our towns and cities, and addicted to the buzz of interacting with people, solitude is not something we necessarily feel comfortable with. Yet deep down we sense that both silence and solitude are essential to our well-being.

Noise pollution has been found to increase the likelihood of stress, high blood pressure, and heart attacks. Our sleep patterns can be disrupted, we become mentally fatigued, and we may struggle with decision making and problem solving. When we hit a major difficulty in our lives, we are more likely to become depressed and feel despair.

Increasingly, many of us are trying to create some silence and solitude in our lives. Ideally, we need to set aside time each day if we can to spend twenty to thirty minutes somewhere quiet—in a garden, a park, or in nature if we're fortunate enough to have access to the countryside. If that's not possible for us, then perhaps we can create a dedicated space in a quiet corner of our house or apartment with some natural elements like a bamboo screen, some plants, rocks and stones, and water if possible, or even a recording of rain falling, the sound of the sea, or a babbling stream—all of which may help give some benefits if we sit quietly on a chair, yoga mat, or meditation cushion. As the writer Pico Iyer reminds us:

> In an age of distraction, nothing can feel more luxurious than paying attention, and in an age of constant movement, nothing is more urgent than sitting still.

If we can find time to sit still and pay attention on a regular basis, we release the tensions in both our bodies and brains. Scientists have demonstrated that a couple of hours of silence daily will even help regenerate brain cells! That may be more difficult to work into our daily lives, but less sensory input is definitely something to aim for.

When we sit in quietness, we tap into our inner world of thoughts, emotions, memories, and dreams. We become aware of an inner voice and hear more easily things that we often ignore. We are more in touch with what we feel and what we think, and this is more likely to result in us finding meaning in our difficult experiences and feeling hopeful about life in general.

Anyone who has experienced enforced silence and solitude, whether on retreat or on some lone adventure, in recovery from illness, or even in exile, or (heaven forbid) captivity, knows something of this. In his novel *The House of the Dead*, Fyodor Dostoevsky writes:

> Sometimes I went so far as to thank destiny
> for the privilege of such loneliness, for only
> in solitude could I have scrutinized my past so
> carefully, or examined so closely my interior
> and outward life. What strong and strange new
> germs of hope were born in my soul during
> those memorable hours!

Hermits, saints, and mystics have always known the value of silence and solitude. So too have writers, composers, and artists. As Franz Kafka, who in his novels explored the human search for understanding, writes:

> You do not need to leave your room…. Remain sitting at your table and listen. Do not even listen, simply wait. Do not even wait, be quiet, still and solitary. The world will freely offer itself to you to be unmasked. It has no choice. It will roll in ecstasy at your feet.

I sit quietly and am aware of my inner world.
I am in touch with what I feel and think.
I listen to the voice within.

5. Practicing gentleness

We tend to associate gentleness with weakness rather than strength. Patience to deal with a situation and achieve our goals requires strength, but gentleness is also a form of strength, just as a stream can eventually wear away the hardness of rock with just a trickle of water.

I learned that gentleness can be strength when I studied tai chi ch'uan. Even though the movements appear balletic, soft, and flowing, they conceal great strength, for they are firmly rooted on the ground and can repel an attacker if necessary. The movements manage to encapsulate the essence of calm and tranquility, but each posture has potent martial arts applications. There is both effortlessness and tremendous power at the same time.

Tai chi chu'an training necessitates patience, persistence, and application, but also demands that you look inside yourself as well as to the body for stability and strength. It develops both our physical and mental capacities and is in essence a spiritual discipline.

The woman that the Burmese call "the Lady"— Aung San Suu Kyi—was until recently revered worldwide for her gentleness and strength. One of the world's great exponents of nonviolence, she was awarded the Nobel Peace Prize in 1991 for her nonviolent campaigning for democracy.

The daughter of Aung San, the general who negotiated Burma's independence from the British, Aung San Suu Kyi had not lived in the country for many years. The military junta seized power in 1962, and in the years before her return to Burma in 1988, she had often wondered how she might help her country. Returning to care for her sick mother and leaving her English husband and their sons behind in Oxford, she found herself in the midst of the greatest popular uprising in Burma's history.

Aung San Suu Kyi chose to form the National League for Democracy and to lead it, campaigning tirelessly for peaceful revolution. She endured many years of house arrest and admits in her autobiography that the early years were the worst, with no visitors, no phone, no money, not enough food, and her husband, children, and friends not available to her. She writes:

> Those who have to tread the long and weary path of a life that sometimes seems to promise little beyond suffering need to develop the capacity to draw strength from the very hardships that trouble their existence. It is from hardship rather than from ease that we gather wisdom.

Aung San Suu Kyi's philosophy of nonviolence is based on firm Buddhist principles. What the West has found difficult is why she has failed to speak out about the treatment of the Rohingya Muslims. The crisis presents yet another difficult situation for her. Caught between a rock and a hard place, she has been lambasted for failing to condemn the violence.

Because she is constrained by the military government, on the one hand, and not wanting to cause a Buddhist backlash on the other, it could be argued that she is patiently trying to achieve the goal she has had all along: to make democracy a reality and to try to get the 135 ethnic groups to live peacefully alongside the dominant Burmese. As a politician, she has to remain strong in the face of criticism, but be patient and gentle in her negotiations, and avoid a return to military rule. She is still well regarded by the majority of the Burmese, and the reproaches of the outside world have united the country in its sense of being misunderstood. Being outside Burma, we are in no position to pass judgment, because however desperate the plight of the Rohingya refugees is, we are not in possession of all the facts; neither are we standing in Aung San Suu Kyi's shoes.

Whatever the rights and wrongs of the situation in Burma may be, coming back to our own lives and the crises we at times face, remaining resolute in our aims, yet at the same time being gentle and patient, is always the best policy. Like the bamboo plant, which is able to endure the burden of winter's snow by bending and springing back when the snow has melted, we have to trust our own strengths and believe in our goals, while being flexible and patient.

I am learning to be both gentle and strong.
Calm and tranquil, I am powerful.

6. Living the questions

There are few easy answers in adversity. A crisis arises, and all is thrown into confusion. We try to fathom why things went wrong or a particular tragedy occurred. We go round and round in circles, wanting to know why such a thing could happen to us.

Sometimes there is no answer; we cannot know why. As the influential Polish film director and powerful storyteller Krzysztof Kieslowski wrote: "We can never see the causes of an event, merely the results. We don't know enough."

Up to this point we may have felt reasonably certain about everything in our life; we knew (or thought we knew) where we were going, but we didn't see the storm clouds gathering. Now, at the moment of crisis, there are only questions.

Our minds continually try to answer the unanswerable. Yet in the end we have to live the questions, pondering them rather than expecting immediate answers. We have to let go of who we thought we were and trust that we will come to see the truth of things and the way forward in due course. We have to accept our lives as they are now, keeping our hearts open and waiting patiently. All we can do is to carry on living and stay present.

The poet Rainer Maria Rilke puts it beautifully in his *Letters to a Young Poet*:

> I want to beg you, as much as I can, to be patient toward all that is unsolved in your heart and try to love *the questions themselves* like locked rooms and like books that are written in a very foreign tongue. Do not now seek the answers which cannot be given you because you would not be able to live them. And the point is, to live everything. *Live* the questions now. Perhaps you will then gradually, without noticing it, live along some distant day into the answer.

It takes time to learn to live the questions, to find that inner strength, just to be curious and to listen, to live with not knowing the answer, to have no certitude. We have to surrender to not-knowing. As the theologian Thomas Merton described it:

> You do not need to know precisely what is happening, or exactly where it is all going. What you need is to recognize the possibilities and

challenges offered by the present moment, and to embrace them with courage, faith and hope.

Ultimately, we emerge from whatever crisis occurred, and we will find ourselves changed by it. With hope, with patience, and living through the questions, we come to see that life can be full and happy, even though it may be different from what we had once thought it would be.

Life's unpredictability changed things for Joni Eareckson Tada in a moment and left her with only questions initially. A vivacious, carefree, and athletic teenager, she dived into the water at Chesapeake Bay and crashed into a rock. She suffered a severe spinal cord injury, which left her paralyzed from the shoulders down, without the use of her hands and legs. She was devastated and her hopes for the future dashed. Bitter and despairing, she begged her friends to help her die:

> Most of the questions I asked, in the early days of my paralysis, were questions voiced out of a clenched fist, an emotional release, an outburst of anger. I don't know how sincere my questions really were. I was just angry. But after many months those clench fist questions became

questions of a searching heart. I sincerely and honestly wanted to find answers.

Joni's faith in God was severely shaken. Why had all the good things been stolen from her? What did she have to live for? Gradually, her focus changed from demanding an explanation from God to humbly depending on him, like Job in the Old Testament who clung to God regardless of all the horrors he suffered. She began to wonder whether even with her paralysis she could live a full life and love God.

During her rehabilitation, Joni emerged with new skills and a determination to help others in a similar situation. She learned how to paint with a brush between her teeth; she learned to maneuver a motorized wheelchair; and ultimately she learned to drive.

Joni's best-selling autobiography, *Joni*, and the feature film of the same name have been translated into many languages. She has subsequently written many books and also recorded several musical albums; in addition, she has appeared on radio and TV and been interviewed in magazines. She is the founder and CEO of Joni and Friends International Disability Center, and is an international advocate for people with disabilities.

I thought my life had been crushed beyond repair. But with the help of God and my friends, it has been rebuilt. Now can you understand why I'm so happy? I've recovered what I thought would always elude me—life in all its fullness.

I keep my heart open and wait patiently.
I stay present and trust that the truth of things is
 emerging.

7. Listening to and sharing our stories

Each one of us has a story. We need to listen carefully if we're to discover our unique story that only fully emerges over time. We need to listen from the heart, not the head. We ask ourselves who we are and why we're here and how best we can live. I've asked myself these questions at various points throughout my life as shifts and crises have occurred. All of us probably do.

"The Universe is made of stories, not atoms," wrote Muriel Rukeyser, the American poet and political activist who managed to balance in her poetry her anger at injustice with optimism and hope. Storytelling is recognized in every society as a way of making sense of our lives and the world. Through stories we find meaning and purpose in our experiences. When we listen patiently, we begin to understand the threads of our story so that we are authors rather than victims of events. Sharing our stories helps us develop a sense of self and can also be helpful for others. We need to listen to the stories of others too in the same manner. Everyone has a story, and sometimes we don't appreciate just how interesting someone else's story is until we really open our hearts and listen. There are so many inspiring stories from those around us that we discover only when we spend time paying attention to them—in our neighborhoods, workplaces, hospitals, and retirement homes.

Stories lift us up and are healing, making us feel more optimistic about our own lives and inspiring us to action. When we share our stories, it can be a powerful experience for others since we all share in the human journey with its twists and turns and the universal experiences of pain and grief, joy and love. Sharing stories helps us feel connected to each other and to the source of life. We realize we are not alone on our journey. In sharing our stories, we become hope givers to each other.

Singer-songwriter Crystal Goh woke up one morning with no voice. She was diagnosed with a rare neurological condition, spasmodic dysphonia, with no known cause or cure. Imagine how hard that must have been for her. To lose your voice when you're a singer, even temporarily through a cold or flu, as I myself have occasionally experienced, is a horrible experience. No wonder Crystal Goh became depressed—she lost hope of even speaking again.

Two years later, as her voice slowly began to return, she wrote a song, "There'll Be Spring," to remind herself of the importance of hope. But Crystal didn't stop there. She shared her song and story with others and set up Diamonds on the Streets, an organization to help young people who have experienced some kind of crisis, and give them a message of hope. In workshops, the at-risk youngsters share their stories and music in a positive and hopeful environment that does not judge. Reflective communication skills are encouraged, and the organization demonstrates how music opens up pathways to healing. In the process of drawing out the personal stories and helping with professionally recording songs that come out of the experience of overcoming their crises and traumas, the youngsters regain self-esteem. Not only are they helping themselves, but they can also be an inspiration to others.

Instead of becoming victims of our circumstances, we too have the power to become hope givers.

> *I listen patiently to my emerging story.*
> *I pay attention to the stories of others.*
> *I know that I am not alone but am connected*
>   *to others.*

8. Looking at time differently

We have only twenty-four hours in a day, and how precious they are! The older we get, we generally feel that there are never enough, and the days, weeks, months, and years zoom by. How many breaths might we have in a day or a year or even a lifetime? The ancient yogis taught that we are all born with a certain number of breaths as human beings. How infinitely precious each breath is, yet how often do we think about our breathing? At rest, the average person breathes 16 times a minute, that's 960 times an hour, 23,040 times in a day, and so on. How we breathe matters hugely, affecting both our physical and our mental well-being.

When we breathe correctly, our bodies are being supplied with the right amount of oxygen, with every cell in the body receiving it via the circulation process. Our cells constantly need a new supply of oxygen so that they can produce energy. As babies, we take relaxing breaths from deep in our abdomen. As we get older, stress often changes the way we breathe, so that we breathe shallowly, in short, sharp breaths. This can result in panic attacks, and even insomnia and depression, and it may well shorten our lives.

We can't live very long without breathing, though we can live a few days without water and maybe a few weeks without food. It is the essence of life, and when we pay attention to how we breathe, it has a profound effect on our lives. If we lengthen the breath, as in many *pranayama* practices in yoga, we may well be helping ourselves to live longer.

So it's not a good idea to rush and try to cram as much as we can into twenty-four hours and get stressed. We pay a price for this behavior in terms of how we feel right now, and it's possible, if the yogis are right, that there are longer-term implications for our life span.

Time is something of a delusion anyway. It goes slower or faster depending on what we're doing. It certainly seems to run faster as we age and as we become more aware that time is running out. The demands of modern life mean we live by clock time, rather than by the way we actually experience time. We in the West tend to think clock time is what matters, and of course, it does make for convenience— for arriving at meetings on time, catching trains, or visiting someone. The danger is that we tend to let our diaries, calendars, timetables, and deadlines dominate our lives. It's our attitude toward time that is the issue.

The indigenous peoples of Australia, many of the native tribes of North and South America, and parts of Asia and Africa view time differently, living more by biological rhythms. In many traditions too, there are universal cycles of creation and destruction that are bound up with myth, religion, and psychology. In Hindu mythology, for example, there is an endless round of existence, with life constantly renewing itself. Things fall apart, but out of the chaos, something new is always being born. Those people who have a different view of time also tend to view their relationship with nature differently: they live in harmony with it rather than exploiting it for their own ends. They know that all life is interconnected.

We can feel that sense of connectedness when we're still and present in the moment. When our attention is focused on this moment now, we are part of the timeless universe. We feel at peace, untroubled by the mind's incessant wandering. With no harking back to the past or worrying about the future, we can rest in the eternal. As Eckhart Tolle writes: "As soon as you honor the present moment, all unhappiness and struggle dissolve, and life begins to flow with joy and ease." When we step out of the constrictions of time, our stress levels drop and our quality of life and breath is better. We free ourselves from the tyranny of time.

I focus my attention on the present moment.
I'm at peace and part of the timeless universe.

9. Attuning to the rhythm of nature

Society has evolved at an exponential rate over the last fifty years, and we have evolved and adapted to meet the rapid pace of change. Whether in the workplace or in our homes, the modernization of society has put us out of kilter with the rhythm of life. Consumption is the order of the day, not simplicity, and much of our life revolves around it. Information overload means we have less and less time to process what we're receiving, and we have less time for real human contact and for ourselves.

Patience is no longer cultivated as a virtue, and everything is expected to be instant, whether it's communication or home delivery. Deadlines and targets dominate our lives and have to be met. All aspects of daily living continue to change at a rapid pace, and it's hard to keep up, especially if we're not as young as we used to be. No wonder many are stressed and crave escape of one kind or another.

Many of us feel the need to slow down and step off this insane treadmill we find ourselves on. Even in Silicon Valley now, many are adopting an "Internet Sabbath," turning off their devices for some part of the weekend, and many companies have introduced stress-reduction programs and regular "quiet time." We need to pause for rest. Just as in painting and music, the spaces and rests are an integral part of the composition.

Nature never rushes. Everything happens in its own good time. We don't have to fall in with the beat of the drum of consumerism, getting and spending, so that we suffer from what has been termed "nature deficit disorder." We can attune ourselves to a gentler rhythm—that of the sun, the moon, the stars, the seasons. Spending time outside is vital, although currently most adults and children are spending less time outdoors than ever before.

Nature has positive effects on our health, well-being, and happiness. Researchers have found that walking in the forest is very beneficial for stress relief and conducive to better moods in general. In Japan, this is a popular practice, known as "forest bathing." It seems that even brief contact with nature for short periods of time can increase positive emotions and decrease negative emotions and thoughts. The 72-Hour Cabin Project is an experiment by Swedish scientists investigating how immersing ourselves in nature improves both physical and mental health. Wilderness experiences are coming to be regarded as therapeutic. So, too, community gardens and parks. Studies across various disciplines have revealed that feelings of contentment and interconnectedness all increase when we're in nature.

This finding is hardly surprising; we all know we feel better when we're in the fresh air enjoying the sights, sounds, and smells of nature. Cities may be stimulating, but there's nothing like nature to lift our spirits. Some of this comes back to the vibrations of the natural world, which are very powerful and which we sense and tune into. We tend to operate in our overstimulated lives within a narrow bandwidth of consciousness at lower vibratory levels. Because nature vibrates at a higher, more powerful level, it helps our minds to settle and harmonizes our vibrations with those of nature. Our breathing becomes regulated, our heart rhythm stabilizes, and blood pressure is reduced. At the same time, stress hormones, such as cortisol, plummet, and hormones responsible for making us feel happy, like serotonin, are enhanced when we are outside with nature.

For me, gardening keeps me attuned to the rhythm of life, acting as a counterbalance to all the other things I have to do, including spending time in the city. Each month of the year has its gardening tasks, linked to the seasons and prevailing weather conditions. I have to be patient if snow covers the ground, or if there's endless rain, or longer-term drought. There's little I can do but wait until things improve, and get on cheerfully with something else. Suddenly, rain and warmth combine so that everything puts on a huge spurt of growth, including the weeds! If I'm not mindful, panic can easily set in, and a sense of there not being enough hours in the day returns. So I remind myself to slow down, breathe deeply, and focus on what is most important to tackle now. When I pay attention, really looking at how all my plants are coping and where there is a need to tie in, stake, prune, feed, water, or remove those weeds that are choking growth, then I feel in tune with nature, and gardening is a joy rather than a burden. As the gardener, poet, and writer May Sarton wrote:

> Everything that slows us down and forces patience, everything that sets us back into the slow circles of nature is a help. Gardening is an instrument of grace.

I remind myself to slow down and adopt the pace of nature.
Pausing and resting are okay.
My mind harmonizes with the vibrations of nature.

10. Learning to live at a different pace

The competitive society in which we live values success, encouraging us to move fast, get ahead, not miss out, acquire wealth, and spend it. There's nothing wrong with being successful and having money, but is that what we truly want? Most of us know it doesn't necessarily make us happy, but too often, rather than following our inner guidance about how we want to live our lives, we allow ourselves to be molded by our parents, teachers, and peers and perhaps pursue success rather more than we want to.

We may have a very successful life with all the trimmings, and we may enjoy it to a certain extent, but deep down we're not as fulfilled as we would like to be. Rather than rock the boat and risk making a change, we carry on. We find ourselves working harder, trying to please everyone, with no time for our own needs and other interests we might like to pursue. Sooner or later something gives—it may be our health, it may be a relationship breakdown, or it may be some kind of external trauma that stops us in our tracks and causes us to take stock.

For me, it was an external trauma that caused me to rethink my life. I was in New York on 9/11, staying in a hotel not far from the World Trade Center. I was preparing to attend my first meeting that fateful morning, having flown into New York the afternoon before. I was actually facing uptown, by choice, with a view of the Empire State Building, instead of the twin towers. I had the TV on while I was sorting through my papers, so I could not see what was happening outside, but I could hear the commotion and then froze as I saw the newsflash on the screen. Not knowing what to do for the best, I hastily gathered what I needed and exited the hotel just as the first tower came down, and I joined the throng of people running uptown through the floating debris and ash.

I was lucky, of course, to be alive, but I was traumatized by the events of that day and then trapped in Manhattan until I was able to get a flight out over a week later. By the end of that year, I had resigned my job and had begun to live my life differently, as did so many of us affected by that day.

Such change also can happen with a nervous breakdown. A friend of mine runs a very successful business. Married, with two small children, a career, and living in a large, comfortable house with a seemingly nice lifestyle, she suddenly realized everything was out of kilter. While she was looking to increase the size of the business and becoming overcommitted with the spurt for growth, everything became impossible to handle, and her collapse was total. Exhaustion, sleeplessness, no appetite, extreme anxiety, doctor, medication, and sessions with a psychiatrist—all this confirmed that normal life had completely broken down. Fortunately, her husband, family, friends, and colleagues were incredibly understanding and supportive. Eighteen months later life is very different. She is back at work on a part-time basis, with someone else running the show. She is learning to live at a different pace.

The other big life changer is an illness like cancer. So many women have had to deal with breast cancer. Judy Naake is one of them. She had an entrepreneurial spirit from a young age, learning her skills in her father's business in Nottingham, UK. Later, working in the health arena, she had an opportunity to launch a well-known brand of tanning products, and over ten years with a lot of hard work, she built it into the premium brand that it has become.

After a double mastectomy in 2003, Judy sold her business to focus on beating the disease. Since then, she has been involved with a number of charities, generously contributing time and money. She is now serving as the High Sheriff of Nottinghamshire, one of only six women in one thousand years to hold this position. She hopes through this role to make a difference to the lives of others.

Thu Nguyen in San Francisco transformed her life after burnout and various health scares. (Yes, sometimes it takes more than a single crisis to shake us into taking a different path.) Since 2016, she's been the CEO as well as cofounder of Flowzo, which helps local residents and neighborhoods get better Internet services for each other. As a result of a precancer diagnosis, diabetes, and depression, Thu began to use naturopathic and other complementary approaches, as well as meditation, to restore her health. She felt she had been given another chance at life and was determined to make the most of it.

When you truly have time to listen to yourself, get comfortable with yourself, you start remembering why you're here. You start remembering our goal as humans and how we are intricately connected to each other. You start realizing that you can't be at peace if your neighbors are not at peace. There's really no better way to spend your time than on yourself.

Thu, like all of us who have experienced a major crisis, was forced to take stock of her life and make changes so that she relearned the art of living. We adopt a different pace and our perspective shifts so that we come to appreciate every single day. We listen to our deeper needs, to what gives meaning and fulfillment to our lives. Learning to live at a different pace, in a more authentic manner, we can more easily help to give hope to others, enabling them to cope with life's challenges too.

I find time for myself and my interests.
I follow my own inner guidance about what I want for my life.
Living more authentically, I give hope to others.

Cultivating patience

Chapter 6

Opening our
hearts to love

*Love recognizes no barriers. It jumps hurdles, leaps
fences, penetrates walls to arrive at its destination
full of hope.*
—MAYA ANGELOU

When we open our hearts, love and, with it, hope
are awakened from within. The lower, negative
vibrational energies of anger, self-pity, resentment,
fear, or selfishness can be dissolved, and love and
kindness toward ourselves, and others, can replace
them. Love is the highest vibrational energy and can
accomplish almost anything. The more we can keep
our hearts open, the greater the love we feel, and
the more patience, understanding, and compassion

we have for others. When we love ourselves, we are more able to love others in a generous and expanded way. Emmett Fox, one of the most influential New Thought teachers of the twentieth century, wrote:

> There is no difficulty that enough love will not conquer; no disease that enough love will not heal; no door that enough love will not open; no gulf that enough love will not bridge; no wall that enough love will not throw down; no sin that enough love will not redeem. It makes no difference how deeply seated may be the trouble; how hopeless the outlook; how muddled the tangle; how great the mistake. A sufficient realization of love will dissolve it all. If only you would love enough you would be the happiest and most powerful being in the world.

What if we find it challenging to get to this place of feeling love for ourselves and for others? It's not difficult to be kind to those we love and who are good to us, or to people we feel kinship with, or when things are going our way. It's far more of a challenge to be kind when times are hard for us, or when we are shocked by the cruelty, injustice, and violence in our world.

One way of increasing the ease with which we can encourage this openheartedness is to practice the habit of getting back to the heart space, that place of peace and joy that dwells at the center of our being, and connects us with others so that we feel love as a matter of course more of the time.

Research at Stanford's Center for Compassion has confirmed that practicing mindfulness and loving kindness meditation, even for short periods of time, on a regular basis has a physiological effect. Blood pressure is lowered; stress hormones are released; and the immune system is boosted. In addition, researchers found that there are significant positive effects on individual's lives, in how they view the world and respond to it, generally feeling more hopeful and compassionate toward others.

1. Being prepared to be vulnerable

What does it mean to be vulnerable? How can it be beneficial in our competitive, even hostile world?

At our core we're vulnerable because we're sensitive and feel deeply. In order to protect ourselves from getting hurt, feeling the negative effects of rejection, or avoiding shame, we tend to armor ourselves, adopting a persona that masks who we truly are. We might be overly nice and charming when that's not how we really feel. We might throw ourselves into activity, filling our days with arrangements, projects, and distractions. We might be restless and constantly on the move, keeping up with the latest trends so that we seem interesting and well informed. We want to show the world who we think we are; we want to impress, be respected, and be loved.

We're all inclined to do this when we're young and have lots of energy and want to succeed in life. When we can no longer do this, for whatever reason—be it illness, disability, or aging—our vulnerability is exposed. We are no longer as important as we thought we were. We have to face the fact that everything keeps changing, and to be human is to suffer.

We all have to confront our vulnerability. As Brené Brown, a research professor at the University of Houston who has written extensively on vulnerability, wrote: "Vulnerability is not weakness, but the core, the heart, the center of meaningful human experiences." It is the prerequisite to living what she calls the "whole-hearted life." We all need to love and belong, to feel worthy of being loved, and to live "whole-heartedly" means to live a life of courage, compassion, and connection.

When, instead of putting on our protective shield to survive, we adopt a gentler approach to living and allow ourselves to be vulnerable, we're no longer trying to bend the world to our will. When we're courageous enough to allow the person we truly are to shine through, we move beyond our beliefs, illusions, and the story we've told ourselves. If we're able to see ourselves as having intrinsic value as human beings, then our state of mind and energy shift. We are capable of being loved for who we are, and therefore we are more able to truly love others. We no longer feel vulnerable, since we feel deeply connected through the heart to human life in all its shapes and sizes, creeds, and colors. We are more understanding, more tolerant, more forgiving, and feel compassion for all those who suffer.

I have no need to put on armor.
I am prepared to feel vulnerable and reveal who I truly am.
I live my life in a whole-hearted manner.

2. Accepting and loving ourselves

From our earliest years, we are taught to look out-ward. We develop the ability to mold ourselves to what our parents, siblings, and teachers want us to be. By the time we're adult and making our way in the world, we tend to behave how the boss, or our partner, or our family and friends expect us to behave.

We can end up living a life that is not truly our own. We give up on our authentic selves in order to please everyone else, trying to be some perfect image that we have of ourselves in order to fit in. Our self-worth is dictated by what others' opinions of us are. We crave approval and can end up con-fused, hopeless, and depressed when we don't get it.

The pain we feel takes us back to our vulnerabil-ity, which, though uncomfortable, is precisely what we need. With vulnerability comes a softness, which means we are more willing to pay attention to what it is we truly need for our well-being. We stop giv-ing ourselves a hard time by trying to be something we're not. We can forgive ourselves for not living up to the expectations we've set ourselves. We learn to accept all aspects of ourselves, including those traits we don't like and project on to others, like anger, jealousy, selfishness, meanness, and so on. We no longer worry about what others think of us; we are okay as we are, at ease with ourselves, and sense that we are part of the greater whole.

Our belief in our own self-worth is vital, and being connected to the whole flow of life helps each of us attain a sense of ease with the person we truly are. Instead of feeling alone and despairing, we can allow the beauty of the world around us to touch us and inspire us. When we are soft, open, and receptive, we find that hope fills our hearts.

The life I'm living is truly my own.
I have no need to be someone other than who I am.
I am at ease with myself and full of hope.

3. Cultivating tolerance and understanding

We might think in the first instance that we're tolerant and understanding in our personal relationships, and that we behave as loving and caring human beings, but if we look deeper, we find that there is often an element of self-interest in our behavior. We're usually fine so long as our needs are being met, but when those who we're in relationship with disappoint or displease us, we tend to react in a negative manner. We always want the best for ourselves, and when we don't get it, rather like two-year-olds who don't get their own way, we tend to behave badly.

This behavior operates both in our personal lives and also in groups, communities, and nations, and is the main reason we don't have the peace and harmony we long for in the world. However we may try to address this situation, the reality is that little can be accomplished unless we address the issue of tolerance and understanding in ourselves. The respected psychiatrist and spirituality researcher David R. Hawkins wrote: "Simple kindness to one's self and all that lives is the most powerful force of all."

The problem is that we see ourselves as separate rather than as part of the whole. We are preoccupied with what we call "I," the ego—the illusory sense of identity we've created for ourselves from our thoughts, habits, and emotions. The ego thrives on identification and separation, and every ego wants to protect and strengthen itself. We're intolerant either because we fear difference, or because we don't want someone else to have an advantage over us or to take something that might benefit us.

There's a Native American proverb: "True peace between nations will only happen when there is true peace within people's souls." Whether in our own lives or in the world at large, we have to overcome the dysfunctional consciousness that is dominated by ego and find a way to be tolerant, which means having the interests of others at heart if we are to find solutions and keep peace and harmony. As the Dalai Lama, a shining example of tolerance and understanding, wrote:

> World peace can only be based on inner peace. If we ask what destroys our inner peace, it's not our weapons and external threats, but our own inner flaws like anger. This is one of the reasons why love and compassion are important, because they strengthen us. This is a source of hope.

Practicing meditation and mindfulness means we can develop a greater awareness of our emotions, thoughts, and behavior. Ego is unaware, but as we see the ego in ourselves, we begin to move beyond it. As we develop greater awareness, we become more accepting and nonjudgmental, more empathic, treating people in a fairer and more balanced way and improving our relationships with others.

*I am becoming more aware of my emotions, my
    thoughts, and my behavior.
I cultivate tolerance and understanding within myself.
I treat others as I treat myself.*

4. Having a compassionate heart
toward others

If we want to be a good friend to others and give
them hope in times of difficulty, then first we need to
feel okay about ourselves. We cannot help others if
we're not accepting of ourselves. We need to feel the
world around us as a place of warmth, friendliness,
and openness, rather than one of hostility, prejudice,
and alienation. We are social creatures and want to
feel connected to other people, but feeling compassionate toward others still begins with compassion
toward ourselves. We can work on cultivating a compassionate heart by looking for the good in ourselves
and in others.

Compassion literally means "to suffer with."
Mechtild of Magdeburg, a Christian medieval mystic, wrote: "Compassion means that if I see my friend
and my enemy in equal need, I shall help them
both equally." The idea of helping our enemies is

challenging to say the least! We're not always comfortable with compassion toward those who suffer who are not our enemies, and we may try to avoid getting involved. We think that only certain people are worthy of compassion and others are not. However, when we harden ourselves to another's suffering, including those we feel enmity toward, we also limit our own capacity to feel joy. We need to try to extend our compassion from ourselves, outward, as far as we can, until we feel kindness for all.

Practicing loving-kindness meditation is a good way to increase our capacity for extending compassion. Originally a Buddhist practice, it has become popular simply because it is so effective and has been adopted by many who practice mindfulness, regardless of their faith.

To practice, we can sit comfortably but upright so that the spine is straight. We can sit cross-legged on the floor on a meditation cushion or yoga mat, or we could be sitting on a chair, so long as we keep our spine straight and are not leaning back or hunched up. We then focus on our breath, breathing naturally and feeling the breath coming in and going out through our nostrils. We can do this until we feel very connected with the breath, not forcing it, but letting it come in and go out at its own pace. As the breath settles, we can try to imagine as we breathe in, a feeling of warmth and love coming in with each inhalation. We can say silently to ourselves, "May I be happy, may I be well." As we feel that sense of loving kindness toward ourselves, we can breathe it out with our exhalation to those we love, saying silently to ourselves, "May you be happy, may you be well." Then we can do the same for someone we have a difficult relationship with, or someone we don't know but perhaps have noticed—for example, a homeless person living on the street. We can continue with our neighbors, our community, and out into the world, sending it out far and wide, saying to ourselves, "May all beings be happy, may all beings be well."

We are each unique and have our own journey. We need to see the good in others, no matter who they are. We cannot tell others how to live their lives, for we do not know their story necessarily. It's important not to make judgments or criticize if their choice about how to live their life is different from the way we live ours. We never have the right to make value judgments about another, as *A Course in Miracles*, the three-volume self-study course that embodies the perennial wisdom found at the core of the world's great religions, reminds us:

In order to judge anything rightly, one would have to be fully aware of an inconceivably wide range of things: past, present and to come. One would have to recognize in advance all the effects of his judgments on everyone and everything involved in them in any way. And one would have to be certain there is no distortion in his perception, so that his judgment would be wholly fair to everyone on whom it rests now and in the future. Who is in a position to do this? Who except in grandiose fantasies would claim this for himself?

Each of us needs kindness, especially in times of adversity, and we all have so many opportunities to show kindness to others during the course of our daily lives—sharing a friendly smile and hello to someone we pass in the street, expressing words of encouragement to someone undertaking something difficult, running an errand for someone, giving a small gift, sharing time with someone who wants company, and helping someone out if they need a lift or money to buy a ticket if they've lost their purse.

Jean Vanier, founder of the L'Arche communities, has been an advocate for people with disabilities and has helped the weak and vulnerable in society. He wrote:

Opening our hearts to love

Wounded people who have been broken by suffering and sickness ask for only one thing: a heart that loves and commits itself to them, a heart full of hope for them.

Vanier founded the L'Arche movement back in the 1960s, having been aware of people being institutionalized with disabilities, by inviting two men to leave their institution and live with him in Trosly-Breuil, France. "Essentially they wanted a friend. They were not very interested in my knowledge or my ability to do things, but rather they needed my heart and my being." The movement has grown, with more than five thousand members in 147 communities spread over five continents.

By choosing to live with compassion, we give hope to all those who need our help, particularly in times of difficulty. Practical help is one thing that we can give according to our ability to give, but it's when we open our hearts that we will be able to give what is truly needed.

I accept and love myself.
I extend compassion to all beings.
Opening my heart, I give all I can to others.

5. Knowing how to forgive

Daily news that our media bombards us with tends to be a depressing affair, dominated as it is by killing, rape, abuse, and terror, and it's easy to react with outrage, taking sides. We need, however, to try to step back and see that both perpetrators and victims suffer. That doesn't mean we condone whatever violent acts have been committed or that the perpetrators shouldn't be punished. It does mean that alongside the compassion we feel for the victims, we should also try to understand the perpetrators' suffering. What terrible past events have caused them to behave in such a horrendous manner? We have to understand that perpetrators were themselves wounded, confused, and angry, and therefore not able to understand the damage they were inflicting.

Forgiveness is a difficult issue for us to deal with when it concerns ourselves. We probably all struggle, and self-awareness and a willingness to see all sides of a situation, not just our own position, are required. When there is conflict and injury, we tend to blame the other person and feel they should be the one to offer an apology. Our decision to blame, however, only makes us miserable. We have to look at our own fears and misperceptions and recognize the pointlessness of them from the point of view of punishing ourselves. D. Patrick Miller, author and publisher, wrote: "To carry chronic anger against anyone or any circumstance is to poison your own heart, injecting more toxin every time you replay in your mind the injury done to you."

It is possible to forgive everyone and everything that has occurred in the past to hurt us, and it's necessary. It's far more than excusing someone for what they have done that has caused us to suffer. Rather it's about the healing that can take place once we let go of our anger and resentment. If, however, we refuse to forgive, the pain does not disappear but is kept alive so that we continue to feel it. The negative emotions we felt as a reaction have to be released if our peace of mind is to be regained. Even if the other person never acknowledges the wound they've caused, we gain freedom. Forgiveness never means we condone the behavior, but it creates the space inside for us to heal.

In 1986, when Jill Saward was twenty-one, she was raped at knifepoint by two men at her father's vicarage in Ealing, London. She was the first woman in the UK to waive her anonymity, ultimately writing a book about the attack.

Jill went on to set up a help group for victims of rape and their families and became a counselor. She dedicated thirty years of her life to campaigning and raising awareness of rape and sexual violence. She also forgave her attackers. In *Rape: My Story*, she writes: "I believe forgiveness gives you freedom— freedom to move on without being held back by the past."

We forgive in the end for our own sake, not for the other person's. A horrific act may seem impossible to forgive, yet if we cannot, it will negatively affect everything we do and every relationship we have. It is, however, a process and takes time.

Maybe we can follow the brave example of Antoine Leiris, whose book *You Will Not Have My Hate* is a moving memoir of the loss of his wife in the terrorist attack on the Bataclan Theatre on the night of November 13, 2015, in which eighty-eight people lost their lives. Antoine had stayed home to look after his seventeen-month-old son, while his wife, Helene, went to the concert. Three days after her death, Antoine posted an open letter on Facebook addressed to the perpetrators, vowing that he and his son would survive and be happy and that the terrorists would not have his hate. Insistent that his life would not be defined by hatred but by love, Antoine is determined to rebuild his life and the life of his son. "You want me to be scared," he writes, "to see my fellow citizens through suspicious eyes, to sacrifice my freedom for security. You have failed. I will not change."

A Course in Miracles is strong on the theme of forgiveness, of both ourselves and others, and suggests that learning to forgive is our only hope: "Forgiveness is the answer to attack of any kind. So is attack deprived of its effects, and hate is answered in the name of love."

I am willing to see all sides of a situation.
I am learning to forgive all wrongs done to me.
My life is defined by love.

6. Trusting the wisdom of the heart

I have a large red velvet heart, edged in gold paint, pinned above my desk. It reminds me to try constantly to live from the heart. I need that reminder, as it's so easy to get blown off course and get mad, envious, grumpy, whatever. If I'm doubtful, I need that heart to show me the importance of not being confused by what is going on in my head, but to be guided by what resonates in my heart. The heart always knows the answers, and when we live from the heart, we naturally feel more hopeful because fear is driven out.

Often we ignore or suppress our feelings, getting caught up in the machinations of the mind. We sway this way and that, unable to make decisions about what to do in difficult situations. If we listen to what the heart is telling us, we end up feeling the rightness of it, there's greater clarity, and we feel more balanced.

Similarly, if we feel passionate about something we want to do, but doubts and hesitations are thrown up by the mind, it helps to follow the dictates of our hearts. We will undoubtedly meet challenges, but we will feel alive and fulfilled if we pursue our dream. If we believe that the future can be better, we need to cherish everything that is part of life, as Jungian analyst and writer Anne Baring reminds us:

> The heart is about cherishing in every sense; cherishing the time given to us in order to discover who we truly are; cherishing the body; cherishing the lives of the people who have been given into our care; cherishing the planetary life which is the great field of all our endeavours.

Opening our hearts to love

Living from the heart and trusting its wisdom means that we feel the interconnectedness of all life, and our natural response is one of appreciation and caring. When we cherish life, we don't want to harm it. We want to trust the heart in finding a peaceful way of resolving differences with our fellow human beings; we want to ensure we do all we can to preserve all forms of life; we want the best for others, both now and for future generations.

I listen to the guidance of my heart and trust its wisdom.
I cherish life and want the best for all.

7. Valuing connection

We cannot live in isolation. We are connected to each other and need relationships to flourish. Although we need to make that journey inward to live from the heart and to find our source of peace and joy, we are at the same time compelled to journey outward to connect with others. The analogy of the spoked wheel is helpful: each life is a separate and unique spoke, but we are all connected at the hub, the center of the wheel. We are connected through heart and feeling.

When we're fearful, we shut down; we don't want to be open-hearted, because we want to protect ourselves from getting hurt in any way. We want to be safe from getting entangled in others' issues and preserve our own sanity. We cannot avoid this, however; life can be a messy business. We need to embrace others as part of our well-being, and that means getting involved.

Families are the great testing ground for connection. They are not always the easiest places, maybe because of unhappy childhoods, sibling rivalry, family breakups, or moves, whether in order to escape one's background or through adopting a different lifestyle due to education and career choices. Cherishing family connection is important, however, and always an opportunity for practicing forgiveness if we struggle with difficult issues. Even in the happiest families, there are tensions of one kind or another, so they are always fertile ground for our own growth.

It is in our intimate personal relationships that we are most challenged. These relationships help us to see where we're stuck, acting as a mirror for us and reflecting back those places that are in balance and those that aren't. Many of us have had codependent or compulsive relationships—in our youth especially. We tended to think it was all about finding "the right person," with whom we could have a special relationship. Such a relationship only reflected back to us what we wanted to see; it was a relationship that fulfilled our needs, or so we thought. In such a relationship, we were inclined to love only what the other could do for us and how they made us feel.

What we learned over time was that no one but ourselves can fulfill our needs. Our partners aren't there to make us happy. Only we can do that, and that happiness comes from within ourselves, regardless of what is going on outside of us. Love is a state of being and not dependent on anything outside ourselves.

In a loving relationship, we have to put aside both our selfish desires and also criticism of what we perceive as faults in the other. St. Teresa of Avila, who well understood the human heart, put it well:

> This is to love:
> bear with a fault and not be astonished,
> relieve others of their labor and take upon yourself tasks to be done;
> be cheerful when others have need of it;
> be grateful for your strength when others have need of it;
> show tenderness in love and sympathize with the weakness of others.

Not only do we have our family connections and our intimate relationships, but we are also connected with our friends, our neighbors, and our communities, and through those connections we learn how we are linked to the whole and experience how love can manifest.

I find that singing in a choir is a wonderful way to experience love and connection. When we're singing a great choral work, there is a wealth of connecting threads—the conductor; the various vocal groups of sopranos, altos, tenors, and basses; the soloists; the orchestra; the musical score; the composer; the librettist; and the venue we are singing in. I recently sang in a performance of that great religious work by Handel, *The Messiah*, in a choir of almost a hundred people. We performed in my local cathedral, a splendid architectural gem with strands of history going back over a thousand years. The sense of all these threads connecting and converging, each one related to the other, all of us dependent on each other, was a totally uplifting experience for all of us involved, including the appreciative audience. After such an experience of connecting to the higher vibrations, there is a veritable glow of open-heartedness and love.

Opening our hearts to love

I cherish family connection.
I alone am responsible for my happiness.
I recognize that I am connected to the whole.

8. Enriching the lives of others

I came across a lovely story on sharing and helping others. A farmer grew excellent quality corn and every year won the award for the best corn. One year he was interviewed by a journalist who learned something interesting about the philosophy of the farmer as to how he grew such good corn—he shared his seeds with his neighbors.

"How can you afford to share your best seed corn with your neighbors when they are competing with you each year?"

"Well," said the farmer, "don't you know? The wind picks up pollen from the ripening corn and swirls it from field to field. If my neighbors grow inferior corn, cross-pollination will steadily degrade the quality of my corn. If I am to grow good corn, I must help my neighbors grow good corn."

It's all too easy to hold back from sharing when we live in the competitive society that we do, but as this story shows, there are benefits to ourselves in doing so. We may resist giving, wondering whether we have enough, or whether it's going to be appreciated, or whether it's deserved. In fact, mindful generosity helps transform us: when we give and observe the effects of giving on ourselves and others, we are learning about ourselves.

Of course, it's wonderful to share what we have with others, whether it's what we own or our time or our caring. However, ideally we want to be giving from a sense of abundance and gratitude, rather than giving in order to receive, or giving out of a sense of duty. It's important to understand our motives for giving. When we give freely with an open heart with no reason for sharing except the love from which it arises, then we enrich the lives of others and our own lives become meaningful.

As Kahlil Gibran, the Lebanese poet and mystic, reminds us in *The Prophet*:

> [T]here are those who give and know not pain
>   in giving, nor do they seek joy, nor give
>   with mindfulness of virtue;
> They give as in yonder valley the myrtle
>   breathes its fragrances into space.
> Through the hands of such as these God speaks,
>   and from behind their eyes He smiles upon
>   the earth.

*I have enough of everything and am able to share
    what I have.
I give freely with an open heart.*

9. Embracing life's magic and abundance

At times we may feel as if something is missing in our lives, and we find ourselves looking for it in all sorts of places. We seek pleasure, but the pursuit of pleasure doesn't bring lasting happiness and fulfillment, even when we get what we want. If we don't get what we want, then we feel disappointed and unhappy. But even when we get what we want, we find that new desires arise, or we're afraid that we might lose what we have. We're locked in a kind of scarcity consciousness that makes us constantly seek something outside of ourselves to fill the gaping hole inside us.

Lasting happiness and fulfillment come when we are happy with what we have, when we accept the circumstances of our lives as they are with equanimity. Yes, we may hope for something better for the future when our circumstances are difficult, but we have to recognize that our happiness will not depend on what arises in the future.

As the Chinese master Lao-Tzu counseled some twenty-four hundred years ago in the *Tao Te Ching*:

Be content with what you have;
Rejoice in the way things are.
When you realize there is nothing lacking,
The whole world belongs to you.

The Tao, which can be described as the way of harmony, the way of integrity, teaches us about the process of becoming fully mature human beings and how to find contentment through practicing self-awareness. We are not the center of the universe as we sometimes imagine, but part of something much more vast and much more miraculous too. When we understand that what we truly seek is deep inside us, there is no scarcity, only abundance. The source of life, joy, and peace never drains dry, but is always bubbling over with abundance.

Knowing this, we can remain hopeful, however we're challenged. Every situation in life is a potential opportunity to discover magic and abundance, and if we stay aware, we can make good progress on our spiritual journey.

I practice self-awareness and am content with what I have.

Opening our hearts to love

I recognize that there is no scarcity in this world,
only abundance.

10. Tasting eternity

When we are less enamored of the distractions that proliferate in the world around us and have the courage to turn inward for a while, sitting still and closing our eyes, just focusing on our ingoing and outgoing breath, we have the chance of experiencing a place of calm and hope. As we become more and more aware of our thoughts, emotions, and patterns of behavior, we understand the power of growth and want to go further on this path. As we see changes in ourselves, we spend more time on our inward journey.

We can always connect with this great well-spring at the heart of our being—the Source of Life, God, the Tao, Chi, Spirit, Cosmic Consciousness, the Beloved, the Universe, Divine Mother, Christ, whatever we choose to call it—but in essence the animating presence that is both within and without. We may experience a feeling of being in love with life itself; we can feel creative, energetic, maybe even ecstatic. We find love deep within us and know we cannot lose it—it cannot be taken away from us.

We are connected with the whole of life and are not alone. We taste eternity because we're living in the here and now, not thinking of the past or of the future, and knowing that everything is unfolding as it should.

The great sixteenth-century mystic, St. Teresa of Avila, wrote about this experience toward the end of her extraordinary life in *The Interior Castle*. She came from a privileged family but was something of a wild child. As a beautiful and vivacious teenager, she had a possibly indiscreet liaison with a distant cousin, as a result of which she was sent off to a convent. She decided, however, that life in the nunnery suited her and suspected that it was probably better than marriage. She dedicated herself to prayer and contemplation, and later in life experienced visions and ecstasy. She went on to found convents and monasteries throughout Spain.

The Interior Castle is a classic of mystical literature and describes the path that takes us to this place of love that dwells in the hearts of us all. The soul is guided through a crystal castle of seven chambers. God calls us deeper into the castle until we are finally united with the Beloved in the innermost chamber. Yes, we have to return to the world to be of service to others, but counsels Teresa:

Once you have been shown how to enjoy this castle you will find rest in everything, even in the things that challenge you most. You will hold in your heart the hope of returning to the castle, and no one can take that from you.

I experience more and more calm and hope in my life.
In the here and now, I am connected with the whole
*   of life.*
I can never lose this sense of love.

Chapter 7

Growing in wisdom

We are not provided with wisdom, we must discover it for ourselves, after a journey through the wilderness which no one else can take for us, an effort which no one can spare us.
—MARCEL PROUST

Wisdom is a way of responding to life, a way of being that comes about as a result of our experiences and how we try to make sense of them. Self-reflection, or awareness, is vital, since without it we may not necessarily become wise just because of what we've experienced. We become wiser as we seek to understand what we've been through, though at the same time wearing our wisdom lightly, for we need to recognize the limitations of our knowledge.

Over time, as we practice awareness, we come to see that though we long for certainty, it's something we can never have, for everything is constantly changing and nothing can be held onto. Change is just part and parcel of life's rich tapestry, and as we weave our way through the warp and weft of our experience, we come to fear change less and see that it isn't necessarily bad. When change is forced on us, as it often is in life, shock can initially make us anxious and afraid. Our identity, which we have become so attached to, is threatened, and we may wonder who we really are and where we're going.

Hope is the great antidote on such occasions, and in struggling with unforeseen events and tragedies, we are challenged to dig deeper, to find the resources within ourselves that enable us not only to survive, but to grow in wisdom. It's through adversity that we learn to be courageous and resilient. We're challenged to change our perceptions and attitudes. As we hope more and despair less, our understanding deepens.

We know that when everything is going well in our lives, we don't really grow as human beings— we're happy paddling along downstream, not wanting to think about the possibility that we might hit a rock or a whirlpool, and that our lives might fall apart in an instant. Some life events are, of course, more demanding than others, and it may well take a long time to process them and emerge from the pain. Adversity does help us grow in wisdom, when we reflect on our experience and live with it. With understanding that comes from awareness, we make sense of it and find meaning, enabling us to reach a place of balance where we no longer resist life's challenges, neither are we overwhelmed by them. By the same token, having greater awareness of the smaller happenings or irritations in life (it doesn't have to be a major trauma) also helps us to grow in wisdom as we learn not to be flummoxed by them but to accept them.

I'm reminded of the Sufi story of Mulla Nasruddin, who very much wanted a beautiful garden. He prepared the soil and planted seeds, and the seeds grew, but so too did the weeds, including a fine crop of dandelions. Perplexed as to how to deal with them, he sought the advice from fellow gardeners, who had various suggestions as to how to get rid of them. Nothing seemed to work, however. Finally, he decided that it was worth making the trip to the head gardener at the palace of the sheik to get his advice.

The gardener was a wise man and had given advice to many other gardeners, and likewise suggested various remedies to Nasruddin. Mulla told him that he had tried them all but to no avail. After sitting in silence for a while, the gardener said to Nasruddin, "Well, then, if you've tried them all and the dandelions still keep growing, then I suggest you learn to love them."

When we arrive at a point where we can accept the way things are, rather than what we think they should be, we come to see with new eyes, approaching what we regarded as unwelcome with greater flexibility. We become more confident about life's unfolding process and remain hopeful about what life has to offer us, as well as believe in our capacity to deal with challenges in the future. We come to appreciate the grace that surrounds us and are grateful for all the blessings that life bestows on us.

1. Learning to take the long view

Despair is a form of impatience. We find it hard to wait for things to change, even if we tell ourselves that they will. Some things take much longer to shift than we imagine, but also when confronted with the unexpected, we forget that we can never tell how things might turn out. Yet more change may lie ahead that we could never have foreseen. "We can't stop the waves, but we can learn to surf," as someone put it. We cannot control the ever-changing circumstances, but we can bring a measure of balance to them, and taking the long view is part of this learning. We need to try to see the larger perspective. If we're mindful, we come to appreciate that every situation can teach us and that we always have choice in how we respond. A crisis may seem like the end of everything we've held dear, and yet it may at the same time open doors of opportunity we could never have imagined. Something that appears to be a curse may well turn out to be a blessing, as the following story of the farmer and his son shows.

A farmer lost a cow, and when he told his neighbors, they said, "What bad luck!"

"Good luck, bad luck, who's to say?" replied the farmer.

The following day the farmer found the cow grazing beside a wild horse. His neighbors were full of congratulations, but the farmer replied, "Well, let's see."

His son came home and tried to ride the horse, but ended up being thrown and breaking his leg. His neighbors expressed their sympathy with his misfortune, and the farmer answered in the same manner as previously.

Within a month, war broke out and the army came marching down the road conscripting every able-bodied young man to join them. The son was upset that he was unable to join the army because of his broken leg. "Bad luck, good luck, who knows?" said the farmer.

The following month news arrived that the entire unit had been wiped out in action.

As so often happens with Zen stories, the tale continues with varying twists and turns.

Unforeseen events always require us to stand back and take the long view, remaining open to the idea that change is part of life and that it isn't necessarily something to fear. It's a question of how we look at things. What can be lost never truly belonged to us anyway, and what we cling to can imprison us. When we learn to let go of our fears, habits, beliefs, and expectations, we have a greater capacity to handle the inevitable changes in our lives.

I know that I am learning from every situation.
I accept change and realize that it is nothing to fear.
I let go of all that is no longer helpful.

2. Allowing things to be as they are

"Knowing yourself is the beginning of all wisdom," wrote Aristotle. It is our ability for self-reflection and seeing from different perspectives that enables us to grow as human beings and make sense of our experiences. Gradually, we learn that the best way of dealing with a difficult situation, if we cannot change it, is to accept that it is as it is. There is simply no point in wishing that it could be otherwise, or as it was in the past, and becoming bitter and despairing. Reinhold Niebuhr's Serenity Prayer can be helpful in such circumstances:

> God, grant me to the serenity to accept the things I cannot change, courage to change the things I can, and wisdom to know the difference.

Wisdom enables us to see what it's possible to change and enables us to let go and move on if it's not. If we cannot accept a situation but instead focus on what we don't have or what might have been, we deprive ourselves of the opportunity for the joy to be found in our life as it is. And however challenging situations may be, there are always moments of joy in every life.

At the same time, when we accept a situation that cannot be altered, there is inevitably grief, so we still need to have a caring attitude toward the part of our self that is broken. Just as a piece of porcelain can have genuine beauty in spite of cracks or chips, or a piece of tapestry can still be exquisite even if the edges are frayed, so too we, with all our wounds and scars, are richer and wiser because of what we have suffered.

Sen no Rikyu is revered as a man of great wisdom by the Japanese, and one of the people most responsible for popularizing and developing the idea of *wabi-sabi*, which roughly translates as "flawed beauty." A writer and a poet of the sixteenth century, he was also a Master of the Way of Tea, a set of rituals revolving around the ceremonial drinking of tea in Japan. As a young man, Rikyu studied under various teachers. There is a story of his visit to one master to learn the rituals of the tea ceremony. The master wanted first to test whether Rikyu was ready for advanced learning and so asked him to tend the garden. Rikyu raked the garden so that it was immaculate. Finally, he shook a cherry blossom tree so that some of the flowers fell to the ground.

Rikyu totally understood that there is beauty in imperfection. This is what *wabi-sabi* is. It reminds us that nothing is perfect, nothing is ever finished, and everything is a work in progress, including us.

I am learning to accept what I cannot change.
I nurture the aspect of myself that grieves.
I am a work in progress.

3. Living soulfully

Paying attention to our inner life, being authentic and true to ourselves, and staying present and aware are largely what living soulfully is all about. Spending time with those we love, sharing in an activity we are passionate about, caring and sharing, we create hope. Living in the present moment, we are able to find balance and experience deep joy, and then we have so much to offer others. Heart and soul are inextricably linked. When we live from the soul, we live with love.

When we ignore the promptings of our soul and are drawn outward to pursue things like wealth, power, fame, or pleasure, we fail to find meaning and become discontented. Deep inside we feel that we lack something. So often we live through will; we drive ourselves hard to achieve the things we think will make us happy, but we become exhausted. Striving doesn't bring the result we long for.

Growing in wisdom

There is a purpose to will in that it helps us to survive, but we need to let our soul lead us rather than our will if we are to feel fulfilled. When we follow where soul leads us through the experiences of our lives, then we discover the richness of life as it is in the here and now. The soul is always perfect, and its essence is love. Instead of seeking outside ourselves, we find what we're really looking for inside ourselves.

Allowing ourselves to be moved and transformed by beauty is also what living soulfully entails. Beauty exists everywhere, whether in nature or in the artistic impulse that seeks to express it. Simone Weil, the French philosopher and mystic, wrote:

> In everything which gives us the pure authentic
> feeling of beauty there really is the presence
> of God. There is as it were an incarnation of
> God in the world and it is indicated by beauty.
> The beautiful is the experimental proof that the
> incarnation is possible.

When we are touched by beauty, it enables us to feel wonder at life itself. We feel nourished, uplifted, and inspired, and the world seems enchanted. We also feel a deep sense of connection to family, community, and the planet, and we want to honor the sacred bond that connects us to each other and to life in all its forms.

We become wiser on our journey toward becoming fully mature human beings and know that we have a responsibility to the world we live in. Wisdom inspires us not to retreat from the world and its problems, but to ask ourselves how we can participate in healing the suffering that exists all around us.

My soul is always perfect.
I let my soul show me the way forward.
I take responsibility for helping to heal suffering.

4. Developing our capacity for joy

Wisdom isn't about knowledge or achievements, but rather about humility and recognizing that there is much that we do not know. It comes from a place of deep awareness and self-reflection, and ultimately is about how we find balance—how we live our lives with equanimity and compassion regardless of events unfolding all around us. This we become more practiced at when we choose to live with hope and find our own way to become more open-hearted and receptive.

Mark Nepo, the writer and poet, wrote: "Each soul is a living flute being carved by life on earth to sound deeper and deeper song." Singing is a way of expressing and releasing deep emotions, enabling us to give voice to our pain and in the process finding great joy. Of all the arts, it seems to me that music connects us most deeply with soul and yet at the same time also connects us outwardly with the world, enabling us to feel a sense of love and connection with others. Our suffering carves out a deeper container for our joy, as Kahlil Gibran expresses poetically in *The Prophet*:

> Your joy is your sorrow unmasked.
> And the selfsame well from which your laughter
>   rises was oftentimes filled with your tears...
> The deeper that sorrow carves into your being,
>   the more joy you can contain.
> Is not the cup that holds your wine the very cup
>   that was burned in the potter's oven?
> And is not the lute that soothes your spirit, the
>   very wood that was hollowed with knives?

Hildegard of Bingen, the twelfth-century visionary, composer, poet, healer, and abbess known as "the Sybil of the Rhine," well understood the power of music to give joy. Throughout her life she suffered illness and was also no stranger to controversy because of her beliefs. Like many mystics, she saw human beings as the peak of God's creation and as a mirror through which God's great glory is reflected. Her ethereal music has an inspirational uplifting quality. Her melodies are ecstatic, soaring toward heaven like the great cathedrals in which her music reverberated. Hildegard saw her music as a means of recapturing the original joy and beauty of paradise. She wrote:

> The marvels of God are not brought forth
> from one's self. Rather, it is more like a chord, a
> sound that is played. The tone does not come
> out of the chord itself, but rather, through the
> touch of the musician. I am, of course, the lyre
> and harp of God's kindness.

Similarly, the thirteenth-century Beguine Christian mystic Mechtild of Magdeburg, who met with so much opposition that some of the ecclesiastical hierarchy wanted her books burned and who in later life suffered ill health and blindness, wrote:

> The Holy Spirit is our harpist,
> And all strings
> Which are touched in Love
> Must sound.

A very different example of music being a means to transform pain to joy is Kenyan singer-songwriter Jaya Awinja, who says that music helped her overcome severe depression. As a child and teenager, she struggled with clinical depression and was in and out of the hospital. During those years, she was confused as to why she had to carry this burden of depression. When she was fifteen, she tried to escape by drinking and partying. Her life was chaotic, and she attempted suicide on several occasions, cursing life when the attempts failed. Music was her breakthrough. She began writing songs about her experience, which was not easy, for she had to go into the dark and bring out the suffering, but she found music to be a release. The title song on her debut album, *Heart Right Here*, expresses what those who have been in pain have felt: "There used to be a heart right here before the darkness and pain, and I want it back again now." Jaya sings with an upbeat tempo and sounds joyful in spite of the lyrics.

Not only music but all creative activities connect us deeper with soul, and through them we find healing. I have a friend who recently lost her husband. With no formal art training, she has instinctively been drawn to painting since he died. Somehow her grief is being processed as she immerses herself in spontaneous painting, and she is finding some peace as a result.

For all of us, giving voice to our pain creatively enables us to become more whole and to have a greater capacity to experience joy.

I choose to live with hope.
I live my life with both equanimity and compassion,
regardless of what is happening around me.
I feel a sense of connection with others.

5. Realizing grace is always available to us

However we are challenged in life, and whatever adversity we have to deal with, grace is always there for us, even though its appearance may be in a manner we never expected. The word *grace* comes from the Latin root *grata* or *gratia*, meaning a "gift freely given." When we look back on our difficult times, we realize that somehow our needs were taken care of, our burdens were shared, and we were indeed blessed.

One of the most recorded songs of all time is "Amazing Grace." It was written by a former slave trader, John Newton. Born in London in 1725, he lost his mother when he was seven and went to sea with his father, a sea captain, when he was eleven. Later, after a misspent youth, he was taken into the British navy but attempted desertion and was consequently flogged and reduced to the rank of common seaman. While serving on a slave ship, he was abandoned by the crew in West Africa. He was eventually rescued, but on the journey home, the ship was caught in a bad storm off the coast of Ireland and almost sank. Newton prayed to God that he might live. He survived, and that was the beginning of change for Newton. He began reading the Bible, and over time began to treat his slaves more sympathetically. In 1764, he was ordained as an Anglican priest and proceeded to write 280 hymns, including the words of "Amazing Grace." Ultimately, Newton made a public apology for having been involved in the slave trade.

John Newton's story is a dramatic one, but all of us know that there have been times in our lives when we seem to have been miraculously spared some horror or have been caught up in something traumatic that went on to be life changing. For Ray and Moth Winn, grace certainly played a part in their changed lives. In 2013, they lost their home after a court battle, having invested in a friend's business which collapsed. At the same time, Moth was diagnosed with a terminal degenerative disease. With only £50 between them, they set out to walk the 630-mile coastal path along the southwest of the UK. Today Moth has outlived his diagnosis and has retrained and qualified as a horticulturalist. Ray, never having written before, has had her book, *The Salt Path* published, in which she tells their story. She says: "When I started out, the grief, pain, and anxiety felt like jagged boulders in my hand. By the end, it felt more like sea-smoothed pebbles and was just easier to carry."

Grace is always there—we just have to open our eyes to it. As the great Bengali mystic and yogi Ramakrishna wrote: "The winds of grace blow all the time; you have only to set your sails."

I know that my needs are always taken care of.
I am indeed blessed by grace.

6. Valuing the power of detachment

As we make our journey through life with all its crossroads and choices, we begin to understand that all those things we thought important and were attached to—our appearance, our role, our ambitions, and our beliefs—matter much less. They merely make up the identity we've built for ourselves, rather than being the essence of who we truly are. They are, in fact, manifestations of our ego, which at a certain stage of our development does need to be strong for us to make our way in the world. Yet in the end, our ego is not who we are, and when a crisis arises in our life, it's the ego that suffers. We have the opportunity, however, to let go of what we've become attached to so that we can find that deeper source of well-being that exists at the core of our being.

Detachment naturally happens as we age, which is why many people in their sixties and seventies, providing they are blessed with good health, are more contented than they were earlier in their lives. By this stage of life, there is less attachment to becoming who we thought we should be and a greater acceptance of the person we have become. We're comfortable in our own skin. We know that the bloom of youth and the energy of our younger days can never be recaptured however much we try to keep fit and eat healthily. We find our once-wider network of contacts begins to fall away and what matters to us are the family and friends and the experiences we share with others who are like-minded. Learning to be a person of no importance is salutary, and detachment comes naturally. We can focus on our inner life and those things that promote our well-being. We have nothing to prove, and we can just practice being instead of doing.

> *I am learning the art of detachment.*
> *I accept the person I have become.*
> *I practice being instead of doing.*

7. Trusting the unfolding of our lives

When we reflect on our lives and all the challenges and dramas we've survived, we are more hopeful that we can weather future storms, with less resistance and therefore less pain. There is no need for us to suffer as we once did. We understand that much of our suffering was due to choices we made, though there is no need to be judgmental about ourselves either.

The lives of others can be an inspiration to us in that they can show us that crises make us who we are and that joy and contentment can follow tragedy and pain, provided we are prepared to look at what has happened with awareness.

Clover Stroud is a journalist who has written movingly in her memoir, *The Wild Other*, about the devastating effect on her life her mother's riding accident had. Clover was only sixteen when the tragedy occurred; her mother was badly injured and brain damaged, although she survived for another twenty-two years. Clover's childhood had been idyllic, but everything changed for her the day of the accident. From then on began a journey of grief, rebellion, and self-discovery. This "wild other" threw herself into a new life of adventures, always around horses, in spite of her mother's accident. She was involved in working with racehorses and then worked on a ranch in Texas. She spent time with a community of Travellers trading horses in Ireland and then traveled to the Caucasus. She lived, on her own admission, on the edge, was reckless, and had a stormy marriage. Clover sees her struggle with grief and trauma as making her the person she is today— strong, contented, in a second marriage with five children. When she looks back on her life, she feels that everything she has experienced has led her to where she is today, able to provide for her children what she herself was searching for—home and love, and a sense of contentment.

Reading the memoirs of others is always illuminating. We see that we are not alone in struggling with what life throws up, and that for all of us our experiences help make us who we are. The poet John Keats, in spite of his short life, was wise beyond his years and wrote with deep understanding, despite his closeness to death, of how the world is "the Vale of Soul-making"—it is through suffering that we learn: "Do you not see how necessary a World of Pains and Troubles is to school an Intelligence and make it a Soul?"

Whether we call it "soul making" or in today's parlance "post-traumatic growth," none of us know how life will unfold. We cannot predict what will happen or the outcome of the choices we make. On our journey, however, we need to trust that when we deal with what happens to us with awareness, in the end we become stronger and wiser.

I am becoming stronger and wiser.
I know that I can survive any future crises.

8. Practicing gratitude and blessing

Giving thanks and expressing appreciation for what we receive from each other is far more than good manners. We know that both as recipients and givers of thanks there is a positive effect. We feel good about it. Conversely, we also know that complaining has a negative effect on us and our relationship with others.

Gratitude is also something that arises spontaneously as a result of the good things that happen to us—it's a natural emotional reaction. It can also be a choice we make—we choose to be grateful and express appreciation rather than just taking something for granted. Maya Angelou understood the significance of gratitude:

> Sometimes I'm overcome with gratitude …
> and feel that each of us has a responsibility for
> being alive; one, responsibility to creation, of
> which we are a part, another to the creator—a
> debt we repay by trying to extend our areas of
> comprehension.

When we feel grateful for what we're experiencing, we sense the source of the goodness in our lives as grace. It helps us to connect—to others and to the creator, nature, the universe, a higher power, whatever term we wish to use. Gratitude is vital, and when we adopt it as a practice, it can help us develop greater awareness. We might want to keep a gratitude journal, writing down perhaps once a week five things that we're grateful for; writing can help us pay attention to the good things in our lives that we might otherwise take for granted. Reading poems and books that remind us about the benefits of being grateful can also be helpful.

Adopting gratitude as a practice has proven benefits, as research by psychologists like Dr. Robert A. Emmons at the University of California and Dr. Michael E. McCullough at the University of Miami have demonstrated. Participants in gratitude experiments lasting ten weeks were more optimistic and felt better about their lives. Other research has confirmed enhanced well-being generally and improved relationships when participants express thanks for kindness.

Even in the most difficult of life circumstances, we can practice gratitude, for it changes our way of seeing ourselves and the world. Dr. Emmons writes about how we have the most to gain when we adopt a grateful perspective at a time of crisis in our lives:

> In the face of demoralization, gratitude has the power to energize. In the face of brokenness, gratitude has the power to heal. In the face of despair, gratitude has the power to bring hope. In other words, gratitude can help us cope with hard times.

Simply spending a little time each morning and evening, giving thanks for all that we have in our lives, rather than focusing on what we lack, and for each opportunity that's come our way with each new day, helps us and all our relationships. Building this time into our lives so that it becomes second nature before and after a meal, a walk, or shared moments with loved ones helps us appreciate how richly endowed we are.

Linked with gratitude is the idea of blessing. Blessing everyone and everything around us makes a big difference to ourselves and others—in our homes, workplaces, shopping malls, stations, airports, wherever we are. Author and personal development facilitator Pierre Pradervand writes in *The Gentle Art of Blessing*:

> To bless means to wish unconditionally, total, unrestricted good for others and events from the deepest wellspring in the innermost chamber of your heart. It means to hallow, to hold in reverence, to behold with utter awe that which is always a gift from the creator. He who is hallowed by your blessing is set aside, consecrated, holy and whole.

Blessing is about intention, about wanting the best for everyone, and it comes from the heart, not the head, from that deep place of love inside us. Blessing everyone is not always easy, but as a practice, we can keep working at it. If we can't genuinely feel it, we can act "as if" we do, and if we persevere, we will begin to feel it.

I am grateful for the good things that exist for me.
I bless all the wonderful people in my life.

9. Honoring the divine feminine

In our culture there is an imbalance between the feminine values of caring, feeling, and intuition and the masculine values of power, technology, and intellect. We have all suffered to some degree from this split. Hope for the future lies in righting this balance so that we are able to honor the feminine as much as the masculine—both as aspects of the divine.

For thousands of years, patriarchy has been the norm, which has meant that men have largely been in control (or sometimes women who have behaved like men). In prehistoric culture there is plenty of evidence from archaeology that women were regarded as equal to men and that there was a greater degree of living in harmony with the world around them.

Although in the Western world, we, as women, have gained considerable independence and freedom, men have continued to have the greater share of power and control and have subjected women to bullying and sexual harassment. In other parts of the world, women are more severely oppressed, subject to violence, trafficking, exploitation, rape, female genital mutilation, and infanticide; basic education is denied many of them.

Fortunately, a shift in attitudes, and hopefully in behavior, does seem to be taking place. There is a greater willingness to listen to what women are demanding. The #MeToo and Times Up movements have seen women speaking out courageously about their damaging experiences. Respect for women and feminine values is something that society worldwide is now being forced to learn. Feminine values have been marginalized for far too long, and we need fundamental transformation of the way we, as human, beings live with each other. Each one of us, regardless of gender, is worthy of respect and dignity.

As we individually begin to live with greater awareness, we can hope to heal the wounds caused by male domination. Each one of us is an expression of the creative life force, which is in essence both feminine and masculine. When we restore the balance of feminine and masculine within ourselves, we can co-create a world of respect, cooperation, and harmony.

When we honor the feminine, it means that we value the wisdom of the goddess. Sophia is the goddess of wisdom (*Hagia Sophia* is Greek for Holy Wisdom). She is the Mother of All, but also another name for the Divine. We can all turn to Sophia for wisdom. All we need to do is open our hearts, and she will reveal herself. She is there when we sit in silence and solitude, she is in the world around us when we are truly present, and she is to be experienced in compassion itself.

I honor both the feminine and the masculine aspects
   of myself.
I open my heart to Sophia, the goddess of wisdom.

10. Seeing the extraordinary in the ordinary

As we begin to grow in wisdom, we not only see the basic realities of life with greater clarity but also see everything around us more intensely. Since we've become more open and receptive, we experience a different kind of seeing. Like the poet William Blake, we can "see a world in a grain of sand," or like the painter Georgia O'Keefe, we can take a flower and if we really look at it, "it's our world for the moment."

When we open our eyes to look closely at something with real interest and curiosity, whatever it is, we see more than we might at first have imagined. It's not a question of needing more time to look at something closely, which we often think is the issue, but rather it's the quality of looking, so that we see as though through a child's eyes, with no attachment or judgment. When we look in this way, we see the extraordinary in the ordinary.

I was moved to read about the Burmese journalist Win Tin, prominent in the late 1980s and one of the founders of the National League for Democracy, who courageously campaigned against injustice and was an inspiration to so many. He spent nineteen years in prison charged with spreading antigovernment propaganda and was released in 2008 at the age of seventy-eight. While in solitary confinement in a cell twelve feet by ten feet, he was not allowed to read or write. He remembered reading in a biography of Van Gogh that while the artist was in an asylum, he walked round and round, so Win Tin put his sleeping mat in the center of his cell and walked round and round. He recited poems and religious texts. "Day after day I did it. I never became depressed, because there was always tomorrow and tomorrow would be a new day."

Through a metal gate, Win Tin could see the clouds in the sky, so he spent hours observing them, noting the patterns changing day by day, season by season. "Watching the clouds, the beauty of the world, these things made me feel proud, and happy to be alive. I did not feel sorry for myself or sorry for the other prisoners like me. On the contrary, I felt we were living an exalted life."

Such words are humbling but demonstrate what is possible even in the direst of circumstances. All the great religious traditions teach us that life is to be valued and that above all, the present moment is precious. The miracle of now is always available to us. The more we live in the present moment, the more we feel gratitude for all the abundance that life has to offer us. We can choose to recognize the value of what we do have, however ordinary, and when we do, we realize we have enough in our everyday lives. It's entirely up to us to focus on it. We have no need for things to be other than they are at this precise moment. There is no need to chase after happiness and exhaust ourselves in the process. When we slow down, in awareness, and have an open heart, joy is right there in front of us. This is true for all of us whatever challenges we're facing. Life is immensely precious, and we need to seize the day, never taking it and the opportunities it offers for granted. As the Argentinian writer Jorge Luis Borges put it: "There is no day without its moments of paradise."

I am learning to see as through the eyes of a child.
I appreciate the miracle of this moment.
I know how precious every day is.

Chapter 8

Becoming our best selves

*We cannot separate the healing of the individual
from the healing of the planet. They are one and the
same, because the consciousness of each individual is
connected to the collective consciousness. Although we
are individuals, we are also each a part of the whole.
As we begin to heal ourselves as individuals, we also
naturally shift the consciousness of the entire planet.
And as the collective consciousness begins to shift, we
are each in turn affected by it. Thus, the more people
change their consciousness and their way of life,
the more the world changes; and the more the world
changes, the more individuals change.*
—SHAKTI GAWAIN

All of us have at one time or another struggled with
despair to some degree, yet we've survived, and

our scars are a testament to life and its inevitable wounding. Healing takes time but in the process of grappling with our problems, and with a measure of introspection, we become stronger and have the opportunity to become our best selves. Healing isn't necessarily curing or solving, but a process of becoming more whole—"soul making"—as the poet John Keats described it. As we embrace our brokenness with awareness, transformation can take place. This is in essence what the ancient art of alchemy was all about—the transmutation of the base metals into gold, transforming our suffering into a deeper and richer way of living.

With the change of heart that takes place in our surrendering to the circumstances of our lives as they are, and finding the equanimity that comes with that surrender, we wonder whether there is a way that we can make a difference through our experience to help others. This is the work of redemption, for in helping others, in whatever way we are able, we find a meaning and a purpose in life. As *A Course in Miracles* states, "Those who are healed become the instruments of healing."

In Greek mythology, Chiron was the wounded healer, after being poisoned by one of Hercules's arrows. In depth psychology, "the wounded healer" is a Jungian concept, and it refers to those who truly understand through their own personal experience of suffering that the wound has to be embraced. In so doing, a more expansive and empowered part of us can be born, and we are able to help others heal from that place of understanding.

"Hope inspires the good to reveal itself," wrote the poet Emily Dickinson. In this lies our hope for the future of our world, which so desperately needs our awareness and compassion. We are living through an extraordinary period in human history, one of radical crisis, of breakdown and breakthrough, as I wrote about in *Wake Up and Hear the Thunder!: Finding Hope in a Hopeless World*. We are experiencing the birth pangs of a new kind of consciousness, one in which we recognize the interconnectedness of all life, respecting ourselves, each other, and all forms of life.

1. Shifting our consciousness

To be our best selves, we accept who we in essence are, but at the same time polish ourselves as it were, ironing out those tendencies and habits that are not helpful or that we've become too attached to. We let go of what doesn't work in our lives, in effect shedding our skins, like snakes, and being reborn.

We accept that we've made mistakes, without judging ourselves, for that is how we learn, but we get up and try again, without taking ourselves too seriously. Every experience of suffering can be an opportunity for growth and a gateway to transformation, enabling us to experience the fullness of life.

As the author Gregory David Roberts, in his novel *The Mountain Shadow*, writes:

> Hope … redeems the heart it feeds. The heartbeat of any conscious now is poised on the same choice that hope gives all of us, between shadows of the past, and the bright, blank page of any new day.

Redemption is possible when we shift our consciousness. Our great hope for the future depends on each of us becoming our best selves, as Anaïs Nin, the controversial and experimentalist writer, put it: "I believe the lasting revolution comes from deep within our-selves which influences our collective life." How we think, act, and behave toward others is what matters. As human beings, we need to stretch out our hands to each other. When we become more aware, more caring, and kinder, we help change the world.

Every day I work at becoming my best self.
I reach out to others and show kindness.

2. Appreciating the gift within our difficulties

Our thoughts, words, and deeds create our experience of the world and influence how the world responds to us. We refine our vibrations with mindfulness and meditation, with gratitude and blessing, and in our efforts to live in greater awareness. Since the vibrational effect impacts the whole, not only do we attract more positive things into our own lives, but we are also contributing to the state of the world.

We learn much from the challenges we're confronted with in life, but there's no doubt that some people have an enormous amount to contend with. It's understandable if we suffer a terrible tragedy or disability that we need to grieve. If illness or disability strikes, we might feel sorry for ourselves and perhaps complain that life is unfair. As the Sufi mystic Rumi reminds us, "Where there is ruin, there is hope for treasure." If we can look beyond the immediate pain and see the gift within our suffering, focusing on what it might be possible to learn, then we will be more hopeful about the future and maybe an inspiration to others through our courage.

Laurel Burch had a rare genetic bone disease from childhood and was in pain for her entire life, suffering with over a hundred bone fractures. In spite of this, she became an artist and used her creativity to become a successful businesswoman.

Laurel had no formal art training but had a passion for art and taught herself to paint. Hundreds of products, from colorful enamel jewelry to scarves and ceramics, carry her designs of amazing cats, mythical animals, flowers, butterflies, and hearts, which are derived from her original paintings. Even though her bone disease worsened, she did not give up, even learning to paint with her left hand.

Laurel chose to see her bone disease as a gift: "Being physically vulnerable is in lots of ways a tremendous advantage in terms of human wisdom. My bone disease was my gift." Asked if she had to choose between her artistic gifts and good health, she said she would choose her art—her goal was to pass on the joy she felt being creative and give hope to others. "I live within the vivid colors of my imagination … soaring with rainbow-feathered birds, racing the desert winds on horseback wrapped in ancient tribal jewels, dancing with mythical tigers in steamy jungles."

Each of us has the ability to change how we respond to our life circumstances and to create a life where we can flourish. There is always a gift hidden within suffering if we can but see it. If we can find a way to live a life of fullness, creativity, and compassion, we can inspire and give hope to others, like candles in the dark, throwing out our beams of light. Kindness and willingness to take action help inspire others to do good deeds too, while at the same time making us stronger and more fulfilled with our own lives.

We know from neuroscientific research that when we experience another person engaging in positive behavior, we are more likely to behave in a similar manner ourselves. There is a kind of contagion in kindness, generosity, and gratitude. Professor Jonathan Haidt at New York University calls it "elevation" and maintains this is different from just feeling happy or warm inside. Instead, people are uplifted and motivated to do good deeds for others; they are inspired to be altruistic, thereby creating an upward spiral for everyone.

I am learning to see the gift within my difficulties.
I create a life in which I can flourish.
I am motivated to help others.

3. Becoming alchemists

Like the alchemists of old endeavoring to turn base metals into gold, or trying to find the key to immortality, we can transform our suffering into conscious awareness and joy. As we choose to live a life of hope, pursuing our dreams and trusting life's process, we fulfill our unique purpose. As a result, we feel more connected to others and become more compassionate toward each other with concern for all forms of life and the planet itself.

The modern-day alchemists are the recyclers of trash, reusing what has been discarded and turning it into something useful or beautiful. They too can show us the way of transformation. While our throwaway consumer society generates increasing amounts of waste and landfills overflow, innovative individuals are turning that same waste into blocks for building, or constructing urban farm pods for growing food. The Retrash Project, started by the Australian Nathan Devine, "seeks to inspire and challenge people to think about how we can reuse waste in creative and innovative ways." Turning trash into treasure, the online community formed around the project has constructed a wide range of useful and beautiful installations and objects, from a shed constructed from old pallets, to a cold frame for plants from an old window, or a chair using old paperback books, to bags, candleholders, and light fixtures.

Many artists make recycled art from trash, turning it into something with a new purpose, sometimes of beauty, sometimes for the sheer fun of it. According to a 2015 report, eight million tons of plastic enter the ocean every year. Richard Lang and Judith Selby, with their Plastic Forever project, collect plastic objects found on the beach in California. Each piece is cleaned, categorized, and stored—ready to be transformed at a later date into sculptures, prints, jewelry, and installations.

Similarly, in Oregon, Washed Ashore is a community-based organization that seeks to raise awareness about pollution of the oceans. Artist and founder Angela Haseltine Pozzi creates amazing giant sculptures of sea creatures using rubbish, particularly plastic, collected from the seashore. These sculptures now tour as the Washed Ashore Project, traveling to educate and inspire people to take action in their own lives to prevent contributing further to the global problem.

H. A. Schutt, together with thirty assistants, created "trash people" from crushed cans, computer parts, and virtually anything else he could find. His installations have traveled the world from New York

City to the Great Wall of China, helping to raise awareness and inspire people as to what is possible by way of transformation.

There are countless examples of artists turning rubbish into artworks. Many did not have the resources to go out and buy art supplies, so they became resourceful and looked for whatever trash they could find to turn into something interesting or beautiful or awe-inspiring.

In the same way, we can take the dross of our lives and transform it into something more meaningful, living creatively with an awareness of the interconnection of all life and wanting the best not only for ourselves but also for others, and for the planet as a whole. Living an expanded and creative life, we become beacons of hope to others.

I am transforming my suffering.
I choose to live an expanded and creative life.
I endeavor to be a beacon of hope to others.

4. Rebuilding our lives and finding new purpose

Sometimes a life can be so shattered that it's difficult to see that rebuilding is a possibility. Making it even better than it was before seems beyond the realms of possibility. Yet people do, gaining a new appreciation of life and transforming their suffering into a life of giving hope to others.

Gill Hicks's life was changed in an instant when she was one of more than seven hundred people injured by four suicide bombers in London on July 7, 2005. She lost both her legs from just below the knee, and her injuries were so severe that she was not expected to live. She tells her story in the book *One Unknown*, the label she was given when she arrived in the hospital as an unidentified body.

Before the bombings, Gill had an impressive career in publishing and design, and was a Fellow of the Royal Society of Arts. When she realized she was going to survive her injuries after intensive care, she viewed life differently; she felt she was fortunate to be given a second chance:

> From the moment I was given the option of choosing life, I made a vow: that if I survived I would live a full life, a good and rich life. I vowed that I would never take anything—all that I have—for granted again. I would never forget how precious every single day is.

I have stayed true to that promise. . . . Once you adopt that attitude and apply it to all areas of life, everything starts to look different.

Gill decided to dedicate her life to being an advocate for peace. In 2007 she set up Making a Difference (MAD) for Peace, a platform that connects people globally and encourages us all to do something every day that promotes peace. Although she continues to feel pain and discomfort, she has learned how to adapt, channeling the anger and frustration she felt initially into something positive. She is now a motivational speaker for peace.

I always choose hope over despair.
I appreciate how precious every day of my life is.
I do everything I can to be an inspiration to others.

5. Transforming what is broken

After tragedy, trauma, or loss, we can never return to things as they were before, but with hope and courage, we can rebuild our lives. Just as countries can be rebuilt after the devastation of war, or historic buildings that have become dilapidated can be repaired, or artworks that have suffered damage can be restored, so can we transform something that is broken. The Japanese add gold paint to the cracks of a broken vase so that it is even more beautiful than it was before. So, too, can we transform our wounds into something more meaningful, and our lives can have a different beauty.

Many lives were changed by the atrocity of September 11, 2001. I was in New York on business, staying at the Soho Grand, not far from the World Trade Center when it was attacked. I was caught up in the mayhem and fear as I left my hotel after the first tower collapsed. I realized that I was lucky to be alive, but I was traumatized by the events of that day. When I was eventually able to leave the city over a week later and return to the UK, I began to ponder making major changes in my life. Ultimately, I made changes that enabled me to live in a way that I could be truly happy, focusing on what now seemed more important to me personally. Suddenly, I appreciated just how precious life was and how it could end more abruptly than I had previously imagined.

William Bazinsky created something extraordinary out of what happened that terrible day. A classically trained musician and composer working in experimental media, he had decided to digitize a series of tape loops of processed snatches of music that he had constructed twenty years earlier. The old tapes began to crumble in the process, but he transformed them into the internationally acclaimed music that is *The Disintegration Loops*. Toward the end of that never-to-be-forgotten day of terror, Bazinsky made a video from his apartment of smoldering Lower Manhattan. As he played his newly created haunting music, with its gradual fades, the project had a purpose. It became an elegy for all those who lost their lives that day.

> *I am transforming my pain into something meaningful.*
> *I appreciate how life hangs by a thread and make the most of every day.*

6. Becoming a channel for good

Each of us has the capacity to become a channel for good, a giver of hope. As we live our daily lives in greater awareness, we are naturally more able to spread hope to others—words of encouragement, gestures of kindness, assistance with tasks that may be daunting, small unexpected gifts for no reason, and positive posts on social media to make people feel positive and smile. We may want to use our time and energy for volunteering, or for supporting or helping to raise funds for good causes. Even within the smallest of arenas, we can make a difference and give hope to others.

There are so many wonderful examples, which we rarely hear about, of those who have been so touched by the plight of others that they are prepared to go to great lengths to do something to give hope. Favio Chavez is one of those. An ecologist and a musician, he was working on a recycling project in a small village in Paraguay. He found children literally living on a landfill site and decided to do something about it. He created the Recycled Orchestra. Instruments were made out of landfill rubbish—oil cans, wood, and cutlery—whatever could usefully be shaped and molded into something that could produce musical sound. He then taught the children to play the instruments and make music.

Tuany Nascimento trained as a ballerina and went on to teach. She realized, however, that there was a need to inspire young girls in one of the favelas of Rio de Janeiro to aspire to more than just getting a job and then becoming a mother. She therefore set up Na Ponte dos Res (On Our Tiptoes), a ballet school to teach girls aged four to seventeen how to dance.

Luc Reynaud was moved by the suffering that Hurricane Katrina brought in its wake. Volunteering with the Red Cross, he was assigned to a shelter in Baton Rouge. He began playing his guitar for the kids, and they loved it. Together they created "Freedom Song," which they played to those who had lost so much and were living in the shelter. Eventually re-recorded, the song was adopted as an anthem by Free the Slaves, an organization fighting modern slavery. Luc went on to form his world-soul reggae band, Luc and the Lovingtons, and now provides free live music for people in need in homeless shelters, youth crisis centers, and refugee camps, bringing much needed hope and joy.

Dr. Sarojini Agarwal is now in her eighties. Her daughter died in a road accident in 1978, but while grieving and asking herself why such a thing should happen, she realized that she could perhaps help other young girls who were homeless and unloved. Almost eight hundred girls have now stayed at her home in India and gone on to have happier lives. A real inspiration, Dr. Agarwal is living proof that with commitment, dedication, and compassion, it is possible to be a force for good and help change the lives of others for the better.

I do all I can to spread hope to others.
I can be a force for good in the world by helping others.

7. Making hope a calling

We cannot help but be moved by the plight of those who need help, but we need to be motivated to act. We may well feel that we want to work for the greater good, but perhaps doubt that we're able to make a difference—we don't have the strength, the courage, the energy, or the capability. If, however, we feel called to do something, then it helps to see that calling as part of our journey of self-exploration and growth. We can remind ourselves of how far we've already traveled and how much we have in our lives to be grateful for. It helps to know too that there exists a community of like-minded souls with whom we can share our experience. This may help us make our contribution in whatever way feels appropriate for us. Hope is power, and together we are very powerful. Hope is the great antidote to despair, cynicism, and defeatism.

All over the world women are working together in small communities, using their talents to help create better lives for others. Their compassion manifests in helping with food banks, caring in hospices, visiting in prisons, working with illiteracy, cleaning up the environment, and creating community gardens. As Helen Keller wrote, "Alone we can do so little; together we can do so much."

Karen Washington has spent much of her life helping to green the Bronx, New York's poorest borough. Regarded as "the queen of urban farming," Karen has encouraged and taught people how to grow trees, fruit, vegetables, and flowers in community gardens. When she moved there in 1985, much of the neighborhood had abandoned buildings, rusting cars, and garbage everywhere. Initially, she wanted to make the place beautiful rather than grow food. She didn't know much about gardening, but the Garden of Happiness was a hopeful endeavor to make an oasis of peace from the city streets and a source of pride for the community. Her "impossible dream" was to have a farm and get more African Americans involved in agriculture. Her vision and her connections through her position on the boards of the New York Community Gardening Coalition, Just Food, and the New York Botanical Gardens have resulted in a three-acre farming cooperative in Chester, New York.

*I am willing to contribute whatever is appropriate for
    me to help others.*
*I am empowered by working together with others for
    the greater good.*

8. Transcending suffering and creating joy

Our capacity to be present in today's world and not turn away from the horrors we're confronted with on a regular basis is far from easy. It takes enormous courage to remain open and empathic, and not close down. Our response has to be one of accepting the uncomfortable truth that division, violence, and conflict exist and have always existed. We also have to recognize that we are both part of the cause and the solution. Every one of us shares some responsibility for what is happening, because at some level there is greed, dislike of difference, and the illusion that we are separate from the mass of humanity.

The solution is for each one of us to become our best selves by endeavoring to become more self-aware, more open-hearted, and more compassionate. We have to face the reality of all that is wrong in our world, yet do all we can to care more and bring hope to all those who suffer from despair.

Lily Yeh and her Barefoot Artists have been inspiring suffering communities all over the world with hope. She believes that living under oppression, persecution, or war can be transformed by creating beauty:

The pain of oppression is a huge mental wall, but where we dare to imagine and thrive, there we have freedom and a joy nobody can control. How do we create joy? Through creating beauty.

Lily creates beauty by painting colorful murals as a means of healing and transformation. She works with local coordinators in war-torn areas like Palestine and Rwanda to work with the young to paint and decorate buildings and homes in brilliant colors, using images from their everyday life as well as from folk art, or simple geometric shapes.

The conductor Daniel Barenboim (together with the late academic Edward Said) founded the West-Eastern Divan Orchestra in 1999 for young musicians from the Middle East, with the aim of promoting mutual respect and understanding through playing music together. Daniel regards it as creating "a platform where the two sides (Arabs and Israelis) can disagree and not resort to knives."

This amazing humanitarian experiment is illustrative of hope's power when people come together in a common bond of shared music against a backdrop of deep political and ideological divide. Wherever the orchestra plays in the world, it gives great joy to audiences.

This was also the case with the great American composer and conductor Leonard Bernstein and his "Journey for Peace" tour to Athens and Hiroshima with the European Community Orchestra in 1985, which commemorated the fortieth anniversary of the atomic bomb. In December 1989, Leonard conducted the historic "Berlin Celebration Concerts" on both sides of the Berlin Wall, as it was being dismantled. The concerts were unprecedented gestures of cooperation, the musicians representing the former East Germany, West Germany, and the four powers that had partitioned Berlin after World War II. As Leonard stated so beautifully:

> This will be our reply to violence: to make music more *intensely*, more *beautifully*, more *devotedly* than ever before.

This was also the response of those artists who performed at the benefit concert held a week after the suicide bomb attack in Manchester Arena at the Ariana Grande concert on May 22, 2017, in which 22 people were killed and 116 injured. The charity concert for the victims' families included some of the biggest names in pop who performed for fifty thousand fans at the Old Trafford cricket ground.

I remain open and empathic to the suffering of others.
I do all I can to give hope and joy to others.
I create beauty wherever I can.

9. Mending the world

The state of the world bewilders us, and we are anxious about what the future may hold. The old institutions in society and politics and economics no longer work, and violence and inequality continue unabated, along with increasing technological change, globalization, and damage to our environment.

Much is changing for the better, however, though there is still a long way to go. Looking on the bright side, we need to remind ourselves of the transformational movements and shifts in consciousness that have occurred over the last sixty or so years, from the civil rights movement, the human potential movement, and the feminist movement of the 1960s and '70s, to attitudes to gender and disability, the rights of workers, and human rights in general in recent decades.

The future, with all its upheavals, may seem chaotic and threatening, but it is also in our hands. We create the future—each one of us—in how we live our lives and with the choices we make. With hope and inspiration as a catalyst, we can act to help mend, restore, and transform our world. Hope means recognizing that another way of living is possible. We can all be instrumental in this change and start to live the way we want things to be.

As the psychotherapist-writer Clarissa Pinkola Estés wrote:

> Ours is not the task of fixing the entire world all at once, but of stretching out to mend the part of the world that is within our reach.
>
> Any small, calm thing that one soul can do to help another soul, to assist some portion of this poor suffering world, will help immensely.

When we consider the history of our world, we know that it is not majorities that bring about change, but committed and dedicated minorities. There is a groundswell of people all over the world right now who see that the old order is disintegrating and something new is being born, and they are choosing to live differently. Each one of us can contribute to the paradigm shift that is happening.

Making hope central to our lives and giving hope to others are vital. As Lin Yutang, the twentieth-century Chinese writer and one of the most influential of his generation, wrote, "Hope is like a road in the country, there was never a road, but when many people walk on it, the road comes into existence."

The inspirational songwriter-poet Leonard Cohen, who reflected our times and the state of society in his insightful songs, wrote in his now famous chorus "Anthem" that everything has a crack in it, nothing is perfect, and it is through that imperfection that we see the light.

Our task is to offer what we can, no matter how small and imperfect our offering. We can choose to remember that love has the power to heal much that needs healing. Whoever we are, whatever our circumstances, we can all try to spread kindness every day of our lives, and help to bring hope to our suffering world.

I play my part in the transformational shift by living as I want the future to be.
I do all I can to spread kindness and give hope to others.
I live in awareness, knowing that I am helping to mend the world.

10. Coming together to overcome the darkness

We have the power to deal with the crises we face, both in our own lives and in the world around us. All we have to do is to start living the way we want things to be, adopting new ways of seeing and being. As Gandhi so famously said, "Be the change you wish to see in the world."

Grace Lee Boggs was a brilliant scholar and philosopher and well-known activist for seven decades, dying at age one hundred in 2015. A radical socialist in her early life, she came ultimately to favor nonviolence like Gandhi, and felt that protest was not the way to bring about change. She spoke instead of a revolution in which we transform how we perceive ourselves, our environment, and our institutions, and as one in which we are all leaders. She believed that we can change the way we relate individually and collectively to each other and can only change society by seeing ourselves as belonging to it and taking responsibility for changing it by "visionary organizing." Having founded cooperatives and community groups in Detroit where she lived, in her later years she collaborated with activists to create a new generation of leaders, starting with inner-city kids. Grace certainly gave hope to many who had fallen on hard times in Detroit.

Hope is about imagining better, about knowing that we are one with the power that sustains the universe, and being free from the illusion that we're separate and not part of the whole. We can no longer think of our own needs without appreciating how we are all connected—the whole human race, all forms of life, as well as future generations. Coming together as human beings, we can create something better for the future. By becoming our best selves, by never giving up on hope, and being aware and compassionate, we are more able to help others. If others lose hope, then we have to find a way to reawaken it, for the miracle of hope is that it's contagious—it's a gift we can give to others.

Our hope for this better world means cooperation in the continual process of change and adaptation. We cannot survive alone. We need living networks as in nature, where all the major ecosystems are built on conversations between the interdependent parts. Our task as human beings is to come together to form a planetary community, overcoming the growing fragmentation and separation. Each one of us can join with another, and then another, so that a revolution in consciousness can come about, as Pope Francis reminded us in his April 2017 TED Talk:

> Through the darkness of today's conflicts, each and every one of us can become a bright candle, a reminder that light will overcome darkness, and never the other way around.
>
> A single individual is enough for hope to exist, and that individual can be you. And then there will be another "you," and another "you," and it turns into an "us." And so, does hope begin when we have an "us"? No. Hope began with one "you." When there is an "us," there begins a revolution....

I live my life knowing that I am connected to all life.
I am becoming my best self and am able to help
    others.
I know that there is hope and that it begins with me.

About the Author

Eileen Campbell is the author of several books, including *The Book of Joy*. A highly regarded publisher for over thirty years, she worked in various capacities for major publishers including Random House, Rodale, and HarperCollins. Visit her at *eileencampbellbooks.com*.